Isle of Skye

Walks

Compiled by
Terry Marsh

Contents

Walk		Page	🖌	🏠	🚩	⛰	🕐
1	**Scorrybreac and The Bile**	10	Portree Bay	NG 488 438	2 miles (3km)	425ft (130m)	1 hr
2	**Brothers' Point (Ruadh nam Brathairean)**	12	Culnacnoc	NG 515 626	2¼ miles (3.5km)	575ft (175m)	1hr
3	**The Coral Beach**	14	Claigan, north of Dunvegan	NG 232 537	2½ miles (4km)	345ft (105m)	1½ hrs
4	**Oronsay**	16	Ullinish	NG 322 374	2½ miles (4km)	425ft (130m)	1½ hrs
5	**Ardmore Point**	18	Trumpan	NG 225 612	2½ miles (4km)	475ft (145m)	1½ hrs
6	**The Old Man of Storr**	20	A855, north of Portree	NG 509 529	2¼ miles (3.6km)	985ft (300m)	2 hrs
7	**Bioda Buidhe**	22	Bealach Ollasgairte	NG 440 679	2½ miles (4km)	920ft (280m)	2 hrs
8	**Waterstein**	24	Neist	NG 133 478	3½ miles (5.5km)	605ft (185m)	2 hrs
9	**Rubha Hunish**	27	Duntulm	NG 423 742	3¾ miles (6km)	660ft (200m)	2 hrs
10	**An Aird and Dunan an Aislidh**	30	Peinachorrain (The Braes)	NG 524 330	4 miles (6.5km)	590ft (180m)	2 hrs
11	**Beinn an Sguirr and the Waternish Forest**	32	Gillen	NG 267 595	4 miles (6.5km)	770ft (235m)	2 hrs
12	**Ben Aslak**	34	Kylerhea Glen	NG 755 206	3 miles (5km)	1,295ft (395m)	2½ hrs
13	**Coire Chat-achan**	36	Broadford	NG 624 255	5¾ miles (9.2km)	405ft (125m)	2½ hrs
14	**The Quiraing and Meall na Suiramach**	40	Bealach Ollasgairte	NG 440 679	4 miles (6.5km)	1,360ft (415m)	3 hrs
15	**Point of Sleat**	43	Aird of Sleat	NG 588 007	5 miles (8km)	1,115ft (340m)	3 hrs
16	**Ben Tianavaig**	46	Camastianavaig	NG 508 389	5 miles (8km)	1,345ft (410m)	3 hrs
17	**Ramasaig, Lorgill and The Hoe**	49	Ramasaig	NG 165 441	5½ miles (8.5km)	1,165ft (355m)	3 hrs
18	**Blà Bheinn**	52	Loch Slapin	NG 561 215	5 miles (8km)	3,000ft (915m)	4 hrs
19	**The Storr**	55	Trotternish	NG 495 510	6 miles (9.5km)	2,130ft (650m)	4 hrs
20	**Rubh' an Dùnain**	59	Glen Brittle	NG 409 206	7¼ miles (11.6km)	1,180ft (360m)	5 hrs
21	**Marsco**	62	Sligachan	NG 486 298	7½ miles (12km)	2,510ft (765m)	5 hrs
22	**Glen Brittle Forest**	65	Glen Brittle	NG 424 258	9½ miles (15.2km)	1,380ft (420m)	5 hrs
23	**Idrigill Point and MacLeod's Maidens**	68	Orbost	NG 257 431	10 miles (16km)	1,770ft (540m)	5½ hrs
24	**Suisnish and Boreraig**	72	Strath Suardal	NG 617 207	10½ miles (17km)	1,505ft (460m)	5½ hrs
25	**Bruach na Frithe**	76	Sligachan	NG 479 297	8¼ miles (13.2km)	3,050ft (930m)	6 hrs
26	**Glen Sligachan**	79	Sligachan (finish Kilmarie)	NG 486 298	10¼ miles (16.5km)	1,445ft (440m)	6 hrs
27	**Srath Mòr and Srath Beag**	84	Head of Loch Slapin (Torrin)	NG 565 224	11 miles (17.5km)	1,265ft (385m)	6½ hrs
28	**Camasunary-Elgol-Glasnakille**	88	Kilmarie	NG 545 172	11¼ miles (18km)	2,280ft (695m)	6½ hrs

Comments

A gentle introduction to Skye, taking a well-defined path around the northern shore of Portree Bay to a raised beach, and climbing onto the headland of Torvaig, before returning easily through woodland.

A brief and easy wander out to a spectacular promontory with a fine view of Kilt Rock to the north. Perfect for a lazy day, or a picnic in a superb setting.

A gentle amble across gorse and heather scrubland and then coastal machair to the so-called 'coral' beach; perfect for a lazy day, for a picnic among the many nooks and crannies and for a little sea watching.

A gentle stroll across rough pasture leads to a tidal causeway linking mainland Skye to the green island of Oronsay; a wonderful experience (if you keep an eye on the tide).

An easy and delightful stroll around a corner of Skye steeped in legend; a quiet, relaxed approach may well reward with sightings of seals and otters along the coastline.

A steep but short climb to one of Skye's most distinctive landmarks, set against vertiginous cliffs, and with a splendid panorama reaching to mainland Scotland.

Surprise views await those who climb south onto the end of the Trotternish Ridge, and up to the summit of Bioda Buidhe. The views embrace the far north-west of mainland Scotland, and the Outer Hebrides.

Many people visit Neist in Waterstein, few venture out onto the headlands. The moors can be wet, but there is usually a dry line to be found. *The walk passes close to numerous sea cliffs, where care is required.*

Visiting the cliffs overlooking the northernmost point of Skye, this walk also drops in on an abandoned village and passes close by the ancient seat of the MacDonalds, Duntulm Castle.

A simple stroll to a lovely promontory with geological and historical interest; the area is good for birdwatching, too, and likely to detain you disproportionately to the effort involved.

A relaxing and agreeable stroll along forest trails leading to a splendid, elevated traverse of the cliffs of Beinn an Sguirr. Outstanding seaward views, reaching to the Outer Isles. A perfect walk for an easy day.

Suitable for a lazy day, Ben Aslak involves a short, sharp pull over a minor summit before pressing on to a surprise lochan and a splendid panorama.

A lovely circular walk heading into the entrance to Strath Suardal, and visiting the remote settlement of Old Corry; there are intimate views of the rocky slopes of Beinn na Caillich in sight throughout the walk.

A splendid outing to one of Skye's most remarkable places, followed by a roundabout saunter up onto the hilltop above for an inspiring view of the Trotternish Ridge and the far off islands of the Hebrides.

An agreeable out-and-back walk through enchanting hummocky terrain to the southernmost point of Skye; fine views of Rum, and golden sand beaches ideal for a picnic.

A perfect mountain for a day away from the Cuillin, offering spectacular views of the Trotternish ridge to the north, and the islands of Raasay and Rona. Largely untracked, this mountain is rarely visited.

Follow narrow roads to a remote part of Skye, and then take to ancient pathways that lead to a 'cleared' village, before climbing up above sea cliffs. The views along the Duirinish coastline are outstanding.

A time-consuming and demanding ascent to arguably the finest mountain summit on Skye; all the effort is generously rewarded with an aerial view of the Black Cuillin and the great Glen Sligachan.

An exploration of the southern end of the spectacular Trotternish ridge, recommended on busy summer days. The view east and west spans a great canvas of islands and mainland mountains.

The walk to 'Roo' Point is one of the most enjoyable outings on Skye. The quality of the walk to Rubh' an Dùnain, however, increases hugely on a fine day, when the dark mountains are etched against the sky.

A strenuous and steep climb over rough terrain to the summit of one of Skye's most distinctive mountains, which proves to be an excellent viewpoint, especially across Glen Sligachan to the Black Cuillin.

A relaxing tour of Glen Brittle Forest, one that allows changing views throughout of the Cuillin and adjacent valleys. Forest clearance has done much to enhance the views, which maintain interest throughout the walk.

An inspiring and enjoyable linear walk to the finest sea stacks around the coast of Skye, accompanied by splendid views over Loch Bracadale to the heart of the island.

A long and hugely agreeable walk underpinned by a sorrowful episode in the history of the Isle of Skye. Easy tracks, good paths and trails lead across moorland to two deserted villages; some road walking

A demanding but spectacular ascent to the Cuillin ridge, across rugged terrain. A day of clear visibility is essential if the rewards are to be reaped.

A long, linear walk through the finest glen on Skye, flanked by sweeping mountainsides and laced with myriad burns. A spectacular and inspirational experience.

These two north-south glens actually link the east and west coasts of Skye, and provide an excellent low-level walk in an area overlooked by walkers bound for the heights.

This excellent circuit dives into the head of Glen Sligachan with dramatic views of the Cuillin, before following the coastline south to the village of Elgol.

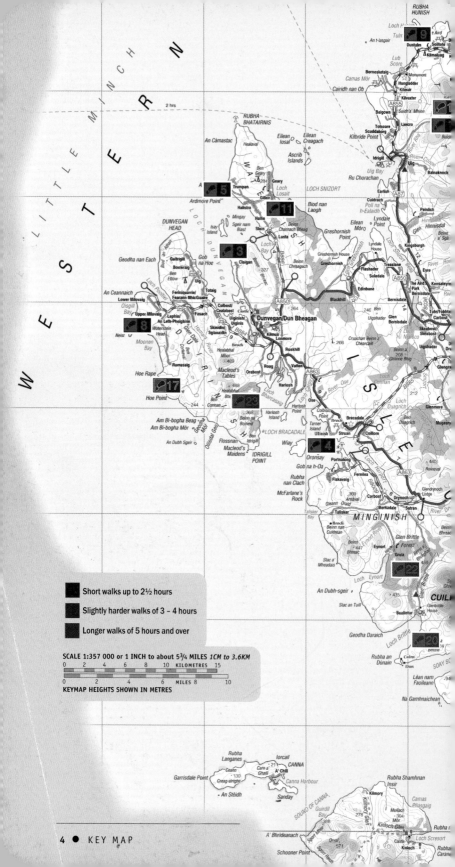

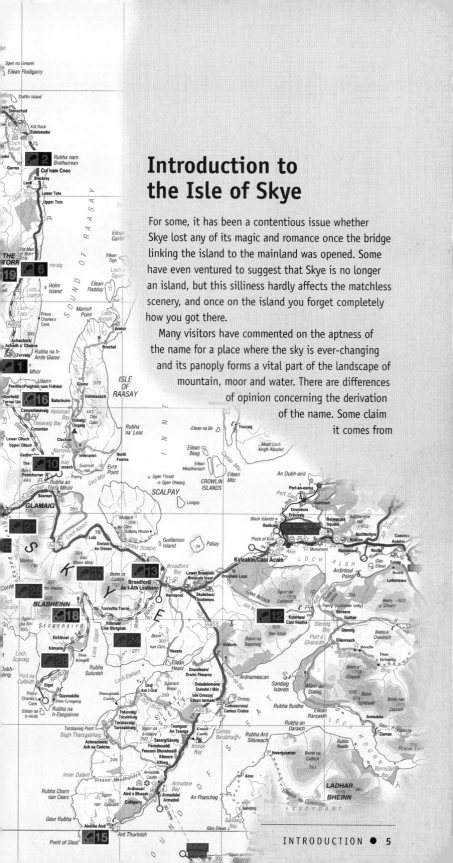

Introduction to the Isle of Skye

For some, it has been a contentious issue whether Skye lost any of its magic and romance once the bridge linking the island to the mainland was opened. Some have even ventured to suggest that Skye is no longer an island, but this silliness hardly affects the matchless scenery, and once on the island you forget completely how you got there.

Many visitors have commented on the aptness of the name for a place where the sky is ever-changing and its panoply forms a vital part of the landscape of mountain, moor and water. There are differences of opinion concerning the derivation of the name. Some claim it comes from

Rowan berries

the Norse and means 'the Clouded Isle', and this would certainly be appropriate in view of the climate, but others think it comes from another Norse word meaning a 'shield'. A further theory puts forward the Gaelic word sgiath, meaning 'a wing', and this may be supported by its appearance on a map. Of course, the island's early inhabitants could not have known of its shape, but once the pioneer geographers came to map the island then the shape will have been evident enough for Skye to become 'the Winged Isle'.

There can be no disagreement about the quality of Skye's scenery. The Cuillin – not the Cuillins, or, worse, the Cuillin Hills – are the heights that lie almost at the centre of the island and form what has been described as 'the most exciting skyline in Britain'. Writer H V Morton described it as '...Wagner's *Ride of the Valkyries* frozen in stone'. Their dramatic outline can be seen from many places across the island. The 'Black' Cuillin, those lying between Glen Sligachan and Glen Brittle, have the most spectacular peaks and ridges and are made of gabbro, a tough volcanic rock loved by climbers and scramblers. Glaciers gouged out the

great corries, which give the ridges and sheer faces favoured by climbers. In contrast, the neighbouring Red Cuillin, to the south east, are made of pink granite that breaks down into scree, which, can be fun to descend, but is most tiresome to climb.

Other landmarks on Skye are almost as distinctive in appearance as the Cuillin. The Old Man of Storr is a familiar sight on the drive northwards from Portree and around Trotternish, an amazing pinnacle that seems to defy gravity and looks as if it is on the verge of toppling. A little farther to the north is the Quiraing, which, like Storr, was formed by a catastrophic landslip during the end of the Ice Age and has similar features. Although the Old Man of Storr is now stable, geologists maintain that the Quiraing continues to slip seawards; if you drive the road to Flodigarry you'll certainly encounter at least one stretch of unevenness where this is apparent.

Rubha Hunish is an unobtrusive landmark forming the northern tip of Skye, a tiny peninsula that can be reached only by scrambling down steep cliffs. It is an intensely beautiful spot that will appeal to anyone with a sense of poetry or a love of wild places. There are many other similar nooks on the island, which lie away from the tourist routes and can be reached only by walkers. The Gaelic has a lovely word for such places, 'grianan', a sunny spot, or a sheltered place for lovers.

Apart from Prince Charles Edward Stuart, Dr Johnson was the most celebrated 18th-century visitor to Skye. His main interest was in the people inhabiting the island and the way they lived, and with typically blinkered vision failed to appreciate the scenic qualities of the island, or had differing standards from today's visitors, remarking: 'No part that I have seen is plain, you are always climbing or descending, and every step is upon rock or mire. A walk upon ploughed ground in England is a dance upon carpets, compared to the toilsome drudgery of wandering in Skye. ...'

This *Pathfinder® Guide* ranges across the whole of the Isle of Skye, a wondrous place and perfect destination for walkers. Typically, most walkers' thoughts of Skye focus on the Cuillin. But there is so much more to Skye as this book will show, providing walks across the island north to south, east to west.

There is an easy division between the type of routes, which are either coastal (or near coastal) or into mountainous terrain. It is among the 'mountainous' selection of walks that the greatest diversity appears, with the walks ranging from demanding routes among the Cuillin to valley ways. Some of the walks are extremely rugged, and involve trekking across untracked hillsides and moorland where the ability to navigate accurately is essential to success. Walks in this category demand proper equipment and clothing and some experience of hard walking: they are intended to whet the appetite of visitors to the region, and to encourage them to explore independently. Elsewhere, the walks visit what I can only describe as corners of Heaven set aside for lovers of solitude and the simple pleasures of Nature: the sort of places where you might well perch beside

a mountain loch watching damselflies going about their business or a grey heron on the lookout for lunch, and become so at one with the setting that you may well not wish to leave. The sound of silence can be a very persuasive argument, and the company of solitude among the most profound of reasons for seeking out Skye's quiet corners.

Walkers whose only experience of walking has been on lowland landscapes, where paths are clear and plentiful or where guidebooks give detailed route descriptions will almost certainly find the area covered by this book something of an eye-opener. Here, some self-reliance is called for from time to time. The ruggedness of the terrain on some of the walks and the remoteness from outside help make this a place where ambition needs wise counsel and the consequences of 'getting it wrong' far more serious. If conditions are poor relax, and wait for things to improve before setting off. Certainly none of the first eight walks in the book is likely to cause undue problems in any conditions, although getting to the start of some

Clach Oscar

of them could be difficult if snow is at a low level. *But the rest need a careful assessment of weather conditions, proper equipment including sturdy boots and a rucksack to carry waterproofs, spare clothes, refreshments, maps and compass.* Even the driest of the walks can be very wet after prolonged rain, and, in Scotland, the rain knows how to prolong. But, to be fair, the sun knows how to shine, too.

Few of the walks are day-long outings; most can probably be accomplished in a matter of hours, allowing time to visit other places of interest. Some are linear, and this will mean resolving the transport problem: two cars are one solution, getting a lift or using public transport are others. Some walks are intentionally 'out-and-back', and these present a completely different set of images on the return journey: others are of variable length – go as far as you want, and then come back.

What many visitors will find fascinating is the incredible richness of wild flowers that prevail here, even high up on mountainsides where I have found heath spotted orchids growing in late September. Around the coast it is the sealife – birds and mammals – that will astound. Nothing will be seen by the noisy visitor, of course, but a quiet approach anywhere could well reward with the sight of deer, an otter, grey or Atlantic seals, whales (even killer whales have been known), porpoise and dolphin, with eagles, golden and white-tailed, appearing overhead.

One final comment concerns the predominance of three wee human-feasting beasties that are an annoyance to everyone: ticks tend to be found in bracken and dense vegetation – if you have a dog with you, do check the dog daily for ticks, which grow rapidly in size but can be removed with care using tweezers; clegs, horseflies intent on aggravating anyone who comes near them and with a ferocious bite, occur everywhere, and then there is the midge, a peculiarly persistent pest that gathers in clouds and munches companionably on all the repellents, creams, lotions and potions used to deter them, generally retreating only in the face of high winds and rain. All of these occur from June until September, but, as the climate has warmed in recent times, this period seems to be expanding.

Setting aside these relatively minor irritations, the walking in the area covered by this book ranks among the best in Scotland. There is a good cross-section of walks to give a taste of everything, and something to satisfy everyone.

This book includes a list of waypoints alongside the description of the walk, so that you can enjoy the full benefits of gps should you wish to. For more information on using your gps, read the Pathfinder® Guide *GPS for Walkers*, by gps teacher and navigation trainer, Clive Thomas (ISBN 978-0-7117-4445-5). For essential information on map reading and basic navigation, read the Pathfinder® Guide *Map Reading Skills* by outdoor writer, Terry Marsh (ISBN 978-0-7117-4978-8). Both titles are available in bookshops or can be ordered online at www.totalwalking.co.uk

The Old Man of Storr

walk 1

Start
Portree Bay

Distance
2 miles (3km)

Height gain
425 feet (130m)

Approximate time
1 hour

Route terrain
Coastal paths;
woodland; some short
steep descents

P Parking
Small car park just
past turning into
Coolin Hills Hotel.
From the A855 follow
the sign to Budhmor

OS maps
Landranger 23 (North
Skye), Explorer 410
(Skye: Portree &
Bracadale)

GPS waypoints
NG 488 438
Ⓐ NG 494 435
Ⓑ NG 497 440

Scorrybreac and The Bile

This short walk takes you round the coast from Portree on a good path that affords outstanding views of the Sound of Raasay and the 1,300 feet high cliffs that form the coastline to the north of the town. There is a continuous path all the way, a delight to follow, leading to The Bile, a remarkable tilted pasture, a raised beach that was formed when the heavy weight of ice was lifted at the end of the last ice age. The route climbs briefly before winding down through woodland.

Portree is the capital of Skye, and its name (Port an Righ, the King's harbour) dates from 1540, when James V visited. St Columba also landed at Portree, and in 1746 Bonnie Prince Charlie, disguised as a woman, managed to evade his pursuers and sailed from the bay, having said farewell to Flora Macdonald at what is now the Royal Hotel.

From the small parking space at the end of the shoreline road (signed Budhmor), take the tarmac path along the shore past a picnic table, boathouse and slipway. Go through a gate, which bears a notice saying that the land belongs to the Clan Nicholson Trust. Scorrybreac, the ancestral home of the Clan Mhicneacall, stood here in centuries past. There are excellent views across the bay to shapely Ben Tianavaig and back to the

The Bile raised beach

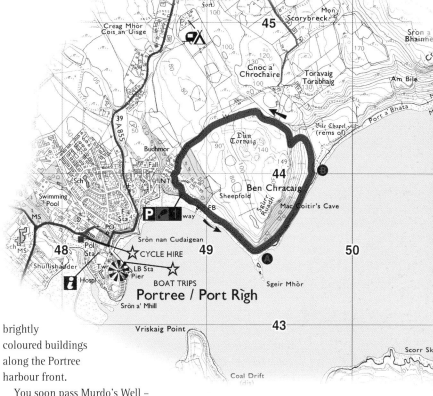

brightly coloured buildings along the Portree harbour front.

You soon pass Murdo's Well – Tobar Mhurchaidh – named after Murdo Nicholson, an active local member of the clan, who restored it. The path is well provided with seats and a viewing platform overlooking Portree Bay. The islet of Sgeir Mhòr is just offshore – a tiny platform of grass surrounded by rocks; it was from here that Bonny Prince Charlie left for Raasay on 1 July 1746. As the path rounds the point  the magnificent cliffs of Creag Mhòr come into view. The path then takes an agreeable course as it winds through thick bracken over outcrops of rock and

loose stones that can be slippery when wet. Finally, you reach a gate ⒷB giving access to the broad grassy, tilted shelf of The Bile.

Do not go through the gate but keep left beside a wall, following a clear path that roughly parallels the wall for a while before turning left and climbing steeply in zigzags through light woodland. At the top, the path levels and presses on eventually reaching three kissing-gates in quick succession. Through the first of these, take a path going left across rough grazing.

Another gate shortly follows, beyond which you descend into woodland once more, twisting downwards and finally emerging onto a surfaced lane. Turn left, and walk down past the Coolin Hills Hotel to meet the Budhmor road, and there turn left again to complete the walk. ●

The Bile

Geologically, The Bile is significant. It is a raised beach, appearing as a distinctive wide, green sward set against a backdrop of lava flows, and displays a well-defined and characteristic tilting along its length, rising from just above sea level to a deep, incised gully below the crags at the southern edge of Sithean Bhealaich Chumhaing.

walk 2

Start
Culnacnoc, Trotternish

Distance
2¼ miles (3.5km)

Height gain
575 feet (175m)

Approximate time
1 hour

Route terrain
Coastal farmland;
rocky shoreline; sea
cliffs

P Parking
Lay-by/parking area
just north of the Glen
View Hotel along the
A855

OS maps
Landranger 23 (North
Skye), Explorer 408
(Skye: Trotternish &
The Storr)

GPS waypoints
NG 515 626
Ⓐ NG 518 625
Ⓑ NG 519 627
Ⓒ NG 525 626

Brothers' Point (Ruadh nam Brathairean)

The brevity of this walk to Brothers' Point, known in Gaelic as Ruadh nam Brathairean, should do nothing to encourage walkers accustomed to more demanding fare to overlook it. This cliff-girt promontory is a splendid detour, something you might tackle at the end of a day's sightseeing around the island, or to go for a picnic surrounded by crashing waves. Take binoculars to scan the waters beyond the Point.

Begin from the lay-by, and walk back towards the turning to the Glen View Hotel, cross the A-road there and stride down a track opposite for Ruadh nam Brathairean (signed: Footpath to Shore). Pass the cemetery and a renovated blackhouse to a gate Ⓐ immediately after which the path turns right, descending along the course of a sunken track. The path curves round and offers a lovely retrospective view of a small waterfall where the Lonfearn Burn splashes over a rock edge in the manner of many coastline waterfalls across Skye. The descending path leads through a gate, and onward towards the bay that has now come into view.

The path runs beside ruined croft buildings towards the shore, but before heading this way, take a moment to visit more croft remains just a little higher, where Taigh Ruaraidh Dhòmhnaill a'Chiurn Ⓑ, tells a little of the small settlement that once existed here.

Continue down towards a shoreline of sea-washed boulders, cross Lonfearn Burn (usually beneath the boulders), and walk on to pass two abandoned buildings formerly used to box and despatch salmon to city restaurants.

Gradually, you rise away from the shore, as you climb gently to round a small inlet on a narrow path that anyone suffering from vertigo may find briefly intimidating. *Children should be closely watched here.* But beyond this hiatus lies a superb platform Ⓒ, a neat grassy terrace with steep cliffs to the south and the continuing promontory of Ruadh nam Brathairean projecting north-eastwards, its lush green sward defended by Dun Hasan, a rocky upthrust thought to be the site of an Iron Age fort, albeit a very small one.

It will suffice for many to stop at the grassy terrace; it is after all a splendid situation, perfect for watching the sun go down or maybe even indulging in a little sea watching. But if you want to continue farther, the onward route lies to the left of a narrow linking ridge, using a narrow path that

Brothers' Point

crosses below the ridge and then clambers onto the small top of Dun Hasan. *The descent on the other side is also steep, requiring care,* but gives onto a superb tip of land of close-cropped turf.

There used to be a cell of early Celtic Christians here – the Brothers, followers of Columba, who gave the promontory its name. All that remains to tell of this is a scattering of depressions in the turf which may have been the location of basic huts and a stone-made cross buried in the turf, although its antecedents may have nothing

whatsoever to do with the Christian community.

To the north, the view takes in the vertical cliffs of Kilt Rock, a rare sea view, and to the south the cliffs of Storr with the hills of the Red Cuillin much farther away. This is a quite captivating spot; if you do not make it across Dun Hasan, simply enjoy the grassy platform to the landward side. It is a lovely place to be. The return is simply by your outward route. ●

SCALE 1:25 000 or 2½ INCHES to 1 MILE 4CM to 1KM

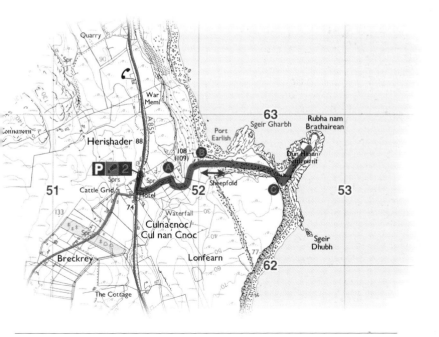

The Coral Beach

Start
Claigan, Waternish

Distance
2½ miles (4km)

Height gain
345 feet (105m)

Approximate time
1½ hours

Route terrain
Broad stony track across coastal fields

P Parking
At start

OS maps
Landranger 23 (North Skye), Explorer 407 (Skye: Dunvegan)

GPS waypoints
NG 232 537
Ⓐ NG 227 539
Ⓑ NG 225 544
Ⓒ NG 224 552

This is a popular corner of Skye, and parking can be an issue at busy times. The walk itself is easy, a gentle amble across gorse and heather scrubland and then coastal machair.

The start of the walk to the so-called Coral Beach is reached by driving past the entrance to Dunvegan Castle, and continuing along a single-track road past Loch Suardal and Loch Corlarach until you reach the isolated farms at Claigan. At a T-junction turn left to a car park.

Walk down through the car park to a gate giving onto a track that crosses rough pasture to another gate, and then parallels the shore. The first part of the route passes round the edge of the small bay of Camas Ban Ⓐ, with fine views across Loch Dunvegan to the westernmost parts of Skye.

When the pronounced track swings right Ⓑ, leave it to cross a small stream and head for a gap in a wall ahead, close by a ruined croft. Beyond the wall, you climb onto a small grassy plateau from the edge of which you get your first glimpse of the

Heading for the Coral Beach

main coral beaches glistening white in the distance.

A gentle descent leads down to the shoreline. Just offshore, the low island of Lampay can be reached at very low tides. After stretches where the shore is all black rock and seaweed, the brightness of the 'sandy' shore is something of a surprise. The fine white sand of the beach is not true coral, but comes from a plant belonging to the red alga *(Lithothamnium calcareum)*. In life this is a rich red colour, but here its calcareous skeleton has been bleached by the sun.

You can return at any time, but a short, steep pull onto the upthrust of Cnoc Mòr Ghrobain  rewards with a view of Lovaig Bay and across to the

Coral Beach

Waternish peninsula and the village of Stein.

The larger off-shore island is Isay, beyond which you can pick out Ardmore Point (*see Walk 5*). Return by your outward route.

SCALE 1:25000 or 2½ INCHES to 1 MILE 4CM to 1KM

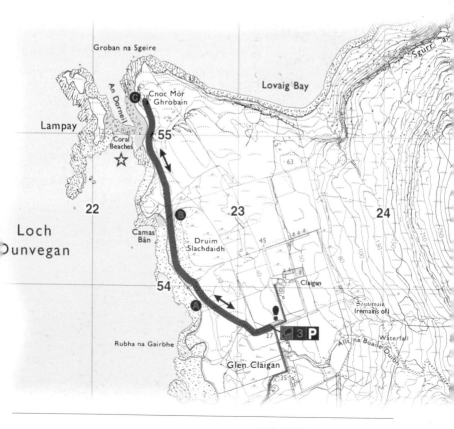

walk 4

Oronsay

Start

Ullinish, Duirinish

Distance

2½ miles (4km)

Height gain

425 feet (130m)

Approximate time

1½ hours

Route terrain

Moorland paths; tidal causeway

Parking

Limited parking area at road end)

OS maps

Landranger 23 (North Skye), Explorer 410 (Skye: Portree & Bracadale)

GPS waypoints

NG 322 374
Ⓐ NG 321 370
Ⓑ NG 319 364

The island of Oronsay is just one of several dotted across Loch Bracadale, but has the distinction of being one you can walk on to at low tide. When the tides co-operate (as they usually do), a trip to the island is a memorable experience. The island is a tilted, wedge-shaped island, rising in a carpet of lush grass from the waters of Loch Bracadale, to vertical cliffs more than 235 feet (70m) in height.

Take the narrow road (signposted: 'Path to Oronsay') that winds around to end near the last cottage in this small, extended, and very atmospheric village; this is a lovely place.

Pass through two nearby kissing-gates, and take to a pleasant track (signed 'Oronsay via Tidal Causeway') across an open meadow, with improving views west and north-west to MacLeod's Tables and the islands of Loch Bracadale.

After another gate and wall Ⓐ – more lovely views abound to entice you – on rounding a small bay the track deteriorates to a path, but is never in doubt, and leads you across boggy moorland to the causeway at Ullinish Point. Go through a gate, and descend a rocky gully to the bouldery beach Ⓑ.

It is important that you cross to Oronsay as the tide is going

Oronsay from the approach path to the island

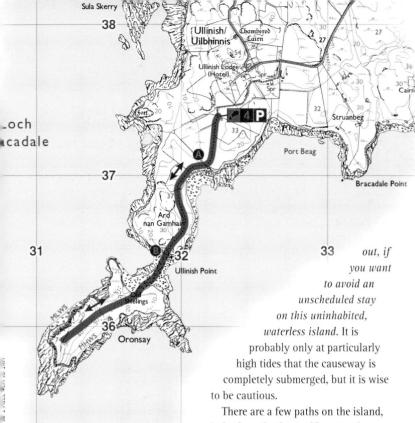

out, if
you want
to avoid an
unscheduled stay
on this uninhabited,
waterless island. It is
probably only at particularly
high tides that the causeway is
completely submerged, but it is wise
to be cautious.

There are a few paths on the island,
indeed one leads steadily up to the
summit, but none is needed. It is a
delightful experience simply to explore
freely, taking in the light at Ardtreck,
the great sea cliffs below Fiskavaig, and
the far, hazy Cuillin, as you work your
way to the highest point. Looking west,
out to sea, the view is especially
interesting: immediately in the
foreground is the island of Wiay, set
against the cliffs of Idrigill Point and
the prominent MacLeod's Maidens. But
much farther out to sea, due west, the
island of South Uist in the Outer
Hebrides lounges lazily on the horizon.
*The Oronsay cliffs come as a surprise,
and there is no barrier against a
spectacular fall in the event of a slip.
So do take care!*

When you have dined sufficiently
on this banquet of peace and solitude,
simply retrace your steps. This is one of
the finest short excursions on Skye,
something to be savoured. ●

walk 5

Ardmore Point

Start
Trumpan, Waternish

Distance
2½ miles (4km)

Height gain
475 feet (145m)

Approximate time
1½ hours

Route terrain
Coastal farmland

Parking
Trumpan church

OS maps
Landranger 23 (North Skye), Explorer 407 (Skye: Dunvegan)

GPS waypoints
◢ NG 225 612
Ⓐ NG 221 611
Ⓑ NG 218 599
Ⓒ NG 218 606

Trumpan Church lies along the western coast of Waternish. Nearby Ardmore Point is the place where Prince Charlie and Flora MacDonald attempted to alight on his crossing from South Uist, and would have done so had they not been fired on by the soldiers stationed there. This brief outing wanders across to one of the most evocative spots on the Island, around the sheltering embrace of Ardmore Bay.

◢ Turn right as you leave the parking area, and go down the hill from the church to a road bend, and then immediately leave the road by turning right onto a descending track. Sheltering below is a power supply sub-station; go past its access and a few strides farther on, as you reach the edge of Ardmore Bay, turn right to walk beside a fence (on your right) to reach and overlook a smaller bay Ⓐ.

On reaching the bay, go left, still beside a fence, climbing Ard Beag and descending to another bay offering a fine view of a double natural arch in the sea cliffs ahead. Eventually the fence ends, and a collapsed dyke leads onward to a more substantial

Island history

The area around Ardmore is renowned in island history for the story of the Battle of the Spoiling of a Dyke.

On a Sunday in May 1578, a party of MacDonalds from Uist landed in Ardmore Bay in a fleet of eight ships under cover of mist, and found their way to Trumpan Church where they surprised the local people, MacLeods at worship. In one of the cruellest episodes in the Island's history, the MacDonalds set fire to the thatched church, burning the congregation or putting any that escaped the flames to the sword, save one. The woman, mortally wounded, escaped and raised the alarm, though the guards at Dunvegan Castle had seen the flames of the church. Vengeance was swift, for the MacLeods, aided by the forces of the Fairy Flag, set about the MacDonalds, and forced them back to the bay, where they discovered that their galleys had been beached by a retreating tide. All but a handful of the MacDonalds were slain, and their bodies lain alongside a stone dyke that was pushed over them as a makeshift grave.

The MacDonalds' act was itself a reprisal for an equally savage act, when the MacLeods found hundreds of them hiding in a cave on the island of Eigg, and suffocated them by lighting a fire at the cave entrance.

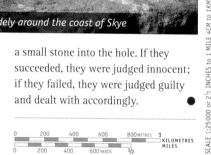

Thrift (Armeria maritima), is found widely around the coast of Skye

SCALE 1:25 000 or 2½ INCHES to 1 MILE 4CM to 1KM

wall close by a group of outbuildings belonging to Ardmore House. Keep the wall on your left until, as it meets a fence, you can pass to the landward side of the fence, and press on to Ardmore Point **B**, always keeping landward of the fence to avoid steep drops to the sea.

Retrace your steps to the point where the fence and wall meet above the outbuildings of Ardmore House, and there bear right, descending to join a broad track **C** heading left around Ardmore Bay to rejoin your outward route near the power sub-station.

In the graveyard at Trumpan Church there is a trial stone – a single upright stone identifiable by a small cup-shaped hole at the top left. Those accused of wrongdoing would be blindfold and required to prove their innocence by throwing

a small stone into the hole. If they succeeded, they were judged innocent; if they failed, they were judged guilty and dealt with accordingly. ●

The Old Man of Storr

Start

A855, opposite the northern end of Loch Leathan, Trotternish

Distance

2¼ miles (3.6km)

Height gain

985 feet (300m)

Approximate time

2 hours

Route terrain

Steep forest paths; rough, rocky mountain slopes

Parking

At start

OS maps

Landranger 23 (North Skye), Explorer 408 (Skye: Trotternish & The Storr)

GPS waypoints

NG 509 529
Ⓐ NG 504 537
Ⓑ NG 502 538

This is a truly spectacular walk, and no one visiting Skye should miss it, but rock fall from the main cliffs of The Storr has occurred in recent years, and the area behind the Old Man of Storr is potentially dangerous. In the interests of safety, it is strongly advised that no one uses the path between the Old Man of Storr and the main cliffs. This popular walk is fantastic in its intimacy with the stunning cliffs of this mountain retreat.

The Old Man of Storr is, after the Cuillin, Skye's most famous landmark. This remarkable pinnacle somehow remained standing when the sedimentary rock over which basalt lava had previously flowed collapsed under the weight. This resulted in some of the most spectacular landslip formations in Britain. The impressive cliffs above the Old Man shelter the surreal hollow known as the Sanctuary, which has more pinnacles and contorted pillars and, as its name implies, is a refuge of tranquility and beauty.

Enter the wood at a gate at the edge of the parking area, and follow a clear track through trees, which gradually thin out as you climb. The path is steep at times, but is well maintained, and a far cry from not so distant days when it was a near-vertical mud slide.

Carry on through the trees until you have your first close view of the impressive rock buttresses of The Storr. The cliff here is made up of at least 24 layers of lava flow, each averaging over 2m thick, with a further 120m of flows buried beneath the scree below. A close look will reveal the Old Man of Storr, set forward to the right of the main cliff, but until you are close enough for it to break the skyline it does not stand out so noticeably.

Continue up the path to a point where, above the trees, you are rewarded with a splendid panoramic view: the Black Cuillin in the south, then the Red Cuillin and Dùn Caan, the highest point on Raasay. North of Raasay, and between here and the mainland, the ancient Lewisian rocks of the low island of Rona (ròn is Gaelic for 'seal') dominate the view (on a good day). Loch Leathan (the wide loch) and Loch Fada (the long loch) stretch out below you.

Carry on past a tiny pool Ⓐ full of bogbean, a three-leafed plant with stunning heads of pinkish-white flowers in

springtime. A short way farther on, leave the forest at a gate and start climbing towards the towering cliffs above. The Old Man of Storr is visible directly ahead, but often blends totally with the cliffs behind.

When the ongoing path forks **B** you have a choice of routes. Either bear right and walk up towards the conspicuous Needle, *but do not go too far as this is a place to which Skye Mountain Rescue are often called out to rescue walkers who have climbed up more than they can climb down.* Or, bear left (the advised route) and follow a clear path to a neat col close by the Old Man of Storr, and with the main cliffs of The Storr directly above.

This is truly spectacular, and should be savoured. There is a clear path heading behind the Old Man, but, if you look closely at the scree below the cliffs, you can see that this is where rock falls have taken place in recent years, and it would be foolhardy to attempt to walk behind the Old Man. Content yourself with being in the company of an ancient 'monument', savour the eerie atmosphere of The Sanctuary, and keep an eye and an ear open for ravens, and ring ouzels, commonly known as the mountain blackbird.

Return by your outward route, taking in the fabulous views across Raasay and the Isle of Rona, and the rugged landscape of Trotternish. ●

SCALE 1:25 000 or 2½ INCHES to 1 MILE 4CM to 1KM

The Storr cliffs and pinnacles

walk 7

Bioda Buidhe

Start

Bealach Ollasgairte (not named on maps); the summit of the pass on the Staffin–Uig road, 3 miles (4.75km) west of Staffin, Trotternish

Distance

2½ miles (4km)

Height gain

920 feet (280m)

Approximate time

2 hours

Route terrain

Rough, mountain walking; moorland plateau; steep grassy slopes

Parking

Bealach Ollasgairte

OS maps

Landranger 23 (North Skye), Explorer 408 (Skye: Trotternish & The Storr)

GPS waypoints

NG 440 679
Ⓐ NG 442 673
Ⓑ NG 438 670

Anyone approaching Bealach Ollasgairte from the west, from the direction of Uig, flanked by the grass and heather slopes of Meall na Suiramach on the left and Bioda Buidhe on the right, might be forgiven for thinking that the latter in particular offered nothing but uninspiring drudgery. Nothing could be further from the truth. Approach from the east, from Staffin, and you immediately get a quickening of the senses, a hint of something special. The Quiraing is a place to get the pulse racing, and renowned for its crazy pinnacles and landslip formations. But few bother with the splendid cliffs and crevices, humps and hillocks that form the landscape farther south, below Bioda Buidhe. This brief walk, up easy grassy slopes, offers views that are among the best on Skye, and simply breathtaking.

From the start, where cars, coaches and mobile burger bars congregate, there is little need for route description. 'Up' might suffice, and for those, mostly tour visitors, who do make the effort, the first stage of the ascent leads to a precipitous and unexpected cleft Ⓐ down which there is a stunning view of the isolated pyramidal peak of Cleat.

Most casual visitors will return from here, but the onward route, always following a clear grassy path, leads gently upwards before moving away from the cliff edges to rise onto a mini escarpment Ⓑ that marks the eastern edge of the summit of Bioda Buidhe.

Bioda Buidhe and the north Trotternish ridge

With the escarpment underfoot all that is required is a relaxed stroll up to the top. But divert frequently towards the cliff edges, or as close as vertigo might allow, and you are rewarded with spectacular images of gully-riven cliffs and raven-clawed corries, lochans and looming land-stacks – Dun Dubh and Druim an Ruma – formed when this part of the Trotternish ridge suffered the same geological fate as the Quiraing.

The actual summit is undistinguished and unmarked, a bare grassy plateau. But to the south, another undulating escarpment leads on to the higher ground of Beinn Edra.

It is easy to pass much time up here taking in the views that embrace the far north mainland of Scotland, the horizon

Cleat from the ascent to Bioda Buidhe

frieze of the Outer Hebrides, and the familiar shapes of Skye, the Cuillin and MacLeod's Tables in particular.

From the summit, simply retrace your steps. ●

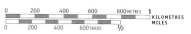

SCALE 1:25000 or 2½ INCHES to 1 MILE 4CM to 1KM

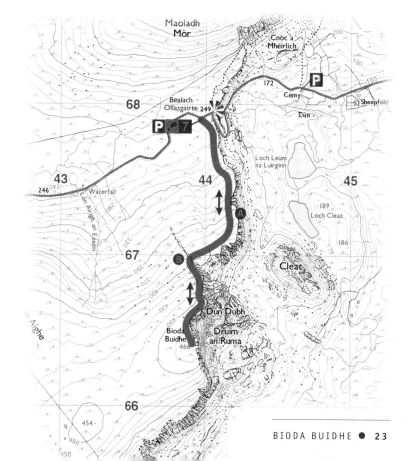

walk [8]

Waterstein

Start

Neist, Waterstein, Duirinish

Distance

3½ miles (5.5km)

Height gain

605 feet (185m)

Approximate time

2 hours

Route terrain

Moorland; coastal margins, sometimes rocky; steep cliffs

Parking

At start

OS maps

Landranger 23 (North Skye), Explorer 407 (Skye: Dunvegan)

GPS waypoints

 NG 133 478
Ⓐ NG 130 482
Ⓑ NG 137 490
Ⓒ NG 138 480
Ⓓ NG 140 477

Visits to Waterstein are usually associated with the long descent to the lighthouse at Neist Point, the westernmost point of Skye, and such a visit can easily be embraced within this walk. However, there is much more to Waterstein than Neist, and this walk takes an elevated trip across moorland to Oisgill Bay, then cuts back towards Neist before descending to the rough and wild landscape directly below Waterstein Head, where you look out on Moonen Bay. So, this is a trip of two bays.

The weight of visiting numbers has meant that the parking area at Neist has had to be enlarged, although it is still not big enough in busy summer months. From the storage buildings at the road end, turn away from the path down to Neist Point, and instead, head north, taking to a track (briefly) and then a grassy path that roughly parallels the escarpment on your left and leads to a disused coastguard lookout Ⓐ.

Continue past the lookout, now following a narrow grassy trod, occasionally indistinct but nevertheless continuous. There are excellent views, left, of sea cliffs plummeting to a raised beach below; while ahead the cliffs rising above Oisgill Bay are hugely impressive.

Pass a small lochan, and press on, always following the escarpment edge at a comfortable distance. Gradually this descends, passing above a large pinnacle, and then allowing

Waterstein Head and Camas nan Sidhean

you to drop to the company of Oisgill Burn, should you wish **B**. A huge rock formation, known as the Shelter Stone, lies down below the cliffs.

Back at the top of the cliffs, turn right towards a fence beyond which you can make out the distinctive domed rows of lazybed cultivation, and beyond this the ridge running out to Waterstein Head forming a skyline. The area beyond the fence is common grazing, but fencelines enclose it unhelpfully. Instead, keep to the right of the fence, trekking across rough ground beside it (keep the fence to your left), heading in the direction of Waterstein Head.

When the fence changes direction, leave it, and head across rough ground, often wet, to approach another fence. Now turn right and parallel this, doing the best you can with the damp going, which persists for a while. Gradually, you approach the last croft in this area, and can pass behind it to gain a shallow gully. Turn left into this and walk out to the road **C**.

By turning right at the road, you can effect a speedy return to the start. But the entire walk continues further. Cross the road just after it bends, and take to sheep tracks heading in a south-easterly direction until you descend into the

gully of the Allt na h-Uamha. Climb easily out on the other side, and resume sheep track tracking as you head into a convoluted landscape of hummocks and hollows. The fall of the land is towards the sea, into which it is all inexorably slipping. Underfoot all is grassy, and when you feel comfortable you can descend towards the small bay of Camas nan Sidhean. A cluster of lava boulders here enjoy the name, actual or fabricated, of Sgeir nan Willie Mhòr – for reasons that will be obvious as you approach. The larger bay out to sea is Moonen Bay, and it was here that Gavin Maxwell, later of *Ring of Bright Water* fame, used to fish for basking sharks.

SCALE 1:25000 or 2½ INCHES to 1 MILE 4CM to 1KM

Walk down towards the shoreline, exploring at leisure, and then take to sheep tracks once more and head back towards the Allt na h-Uamha , which creates a waterslide as it reaches its end. This time you cross the ravine much nearer the sea, above the waterfall, and take to a clear, but narrow slanting path across rocks opposite. This soon leads up to easier ground above, across which you can continue to follow the coast, now above the cliffs, until you can turn up to the starting point at the road end. ●

Sea cliffs, Oisgill Bay

Rubha Hunish

The most northerly point of Skye is Rubha Hunish, a long, grassy peninsula defended by steep cliffs, and ringed by crags and fine sea stacks. Alas, the very northernmost point is far from easy to reach, being protected by the craggy face of Meall Tuath. There is only one way through, and this descends vertical cliffs – not for the inexperienced or anyone suffering from vertigo, so avoid it if you prefer. Rubha Hunish always looks inviting, but the coastguard lookout on Meall Tuath is a more-than-ample target for a walk and a stunning viewpoint.

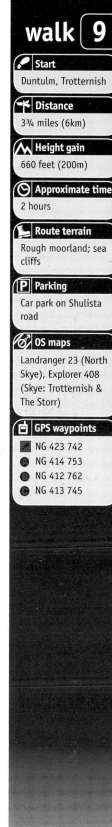

walk 9

Start
Duntulm, Trotternish

Distance
3¾ miles (6km)

Height gain
660 feet (200m)

Approximate time
2 hours

Route terrain
Rough moorland; sea cliffs

Parking
Car park on Shulista road

OS maps
Landranger 23 (North Skye), Explorer 408 (Skye: Trotternish & The Storr)

GPS waypoints
NG 423 742
Ⓐ NG 414 753
Ⓑ NG 412 762
Ⓒ NG 413 745

From the parking area just near the start of the minor road to Shulista, cross the nearby cattle-grid and immediately go left into heather to follow a wet path that is clearly waymarked by white-banded poles. The path rambles on easily enough, along the foot of a minor hill slope with your objective in view ahead. Stay with the waymarked route, to reach the deserted crofts of the village of Erisco Ⓐ.

> **Erisco** The land around Erisco forms part of the North Duntulm township, and used to be an excellent area for growing potatoes and oats. It is thought that the name comes from 'Erie', meaning a low tract of land, and 'Sco', meaning a green open field. During the time of the Highland Clearances, when crofters were being moved to make way for sheep, landlords were forced to resettle their tenants elsewhere, and Erisco was used for this purpose. Eight crofters built thatched cottages along the township enclosure wall at the head of the crofts; there is also evidence, in the form of lazybed cultivation, of an earlier township.
>
> When conditions improved for crofters in the late 19th century, places like Erisco were vacated. An old map of Inverness-shire (1878, i.e. before the Crofters Act of 1886), shows a crofting township of 14 unroofed buildings, one enclosure, a field system and a head dyke. Today, Erisco remains as the best example of a depopulated 'improvements' township in Skye.

Further waymarks steer you up to a wooden gate in a fence. Through this, initially take the left-hand (lower) path, but soon start to climb onto Meall Tuath, finally reaching the former coastguard lookout Ⓑ, now in the care of the Mountain Bothies Association, and used as such. The hut used to be manned around the clock, and is a welcome shelter on a wild day.

As might be expected, the setting is truly spectacular; only a

Duntulm Castle

down to the headland below. It is not a walkers' route, requiring the use of hands and a bit of mild scrambling in places. Without the necessary experience, content yourself with enjoying the panorama from Meall Tuath. But, if you want to go this

few strides away the grassy Rubha Hunish, the northerly tip of Skye, comes into view. Immediately below, but not immediately obvious are the parallel cultivation strips of the runrig (lazybed) system that were farmed here by the people of Erisco. To the north-east, and sporting a lighthouse, is the island of Eilean Trodday, while to the north-west lie Gearran Island, Gaeilavore Island and Fladda-chùain, on which St Columba had a chapel. Beyond these islands, 15 miles distant, are the islands of Harris and Lewis in the Outer Hebrides.

Meall Tuath has a second top, Meall Deas, south-west of the highest point, and between the two, from a heathery ravine, *there is a rocky path slipping*

way, then take care; it looks alarming, but you should soon see a clear path lower down, and even the initial section looks worse than it is. However, you do need to take care as you descend; soon you are free of the rocks and can explore the grassy headland at leisure. This is a great place for spotting otters. If you make a circuit of the whole headland, especially to the eastern side you will find some fascinating little inlets, or 'geos'. There are also three great sea stacks on the eastern side and a natural arch. The cliffs themselves are host during the breeding season to countless razorbills and shags. The very northernmost tip of this headland is arguably the best place on Skye from which to see dolphins, harbour porpoise

Duntulm Castle Duntulm Castle occupies a strong, defensible position on a small promontory to the north of Score Bay, virtually inaccessible from the sea, except through Port Duntulm Bay. The castle was the MacDonald base on Skye from the early 16th century, and has a long and chequered history that embraces both glory and bloodshed. Little remains of the original structure. The MacDonald womenfolk are said to have made a garden with soil brought from seven kingdoms and, looking at the crumbling walls today, it is hard to imagine the great feast given by Donald of the Wars, when 50 maidens danced for him.

There is a local tradition that a fort from very early times, which was demolished to provide material for the castle, occupied the site. For most of the time the castle was in the possession of the MacLeods of Dunvegan, but it is generally accepted that the MacDonalds moved here from Dun Sgathaich around 1539.

It is traditionally thought the MacDonalds left Duntulm just before the Rebellion of 1715, though there is evidence that they were still in residence ten years later.

and whales, especially during the summer months of July and August. Having completed your tour of the headland – the western side is somewhat less spectacular than the east – then simply retrace your steps up the cliff face and turn right to gain the minor summit of Meall Deas.

From Meall Deas, the path continues clearly down to a gate in a fence corner at the edge of Tulm Bay and Tulm Island – this is also a good place to spot otters.

A reasonable, if wet, path now runs parallel with the foreshore, with Duntulm Castle becoming ever more pronounced on its rocky headland.

When the foreshore path encounters a wall 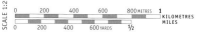, directly opposite the castle, turn inland beside it to a wall corner. Turn this and soon reach a fence, crossed by a step-stile a short distance away. Continue on the other side, close by the ongoing wall, and take the first gate on the right. Bear left to pass a cottage and then reach a row of cottages formerly occupied by the coastguards who manned the lookout, but now seeing service as holiday lets. Walk past these, and the lovely Loch Cleat, to reach the main road. Turn left and follow this for 700 yds to the Shulista turning, and the end of the walk. ●

0   200   400   600   800 METRES   1
                              KILOMETRES
                              MILES
0   200   400   600 YARDS   ½

Rubha Hunish

77

Bodha Hunish

Geodha na Mòine

Hunish

20

Loch Hunish

Port Lag a' Bhleodhainn

Lùb a' Sgiathain

Bun-idein

MLWS

Meall Tuath

76

100

82

ha Voreven

Meall Deas

80

80

90

Rubha Smellavig

eir nan Sgarbh

Lùb Voreven

41

70

60

42

90

Dunvannarain

68

43

Cnoc a' Chlach

Cnoc Riasal

St Mc

Bodh' an Eilean

Duntulm Bay

Erisco

A

60

30

20

Tulm Island

Tulm Bay

MHWS

Port Erisco

75

30

Blàr Stamanaig

40

34

Cattle Grid

Shulista

Ru Meanish

Port Duntulm

C

52

50

Sheep Dip

36

Cattle Grid

9 P

GALLERY

Solitote

14

Duntulm Castle Slipway (rems of)

Hotel

Loch Cleat

38

P

24 A855

74 Duntulm

Cnoc Roll

122

Kilmaluag

Sheep

walk 10

Start
Peinachorrain (The Braes)

Distance
4 miles (6.5km)

Height gain
590 feet (180m)

Approximate time
2 hours

Route terrain
Road walking (quiet); coastal fields and cliffs

Parking
Limited parking at road end

OS maps
Landranger 32 (South Skye & Cuillin Hills), Explorer 410 (Skye: Portree & Bracadale)

GPS waypoints
 NG 524 330
Ⓐ NG 526 335
Ⓑ NG 527 342
Ⓒ NG 532 357

An Aird and Dunan an Aislidh

There is a pleasure about this fairly short walk that is disproportionate to the effort required. This quiet corner of Skye has a place in history, in the island's geological make up and proves to be a fine place for birdwatching, too. Rainy days do not seem to matter here; just take a pair of binoculars and you could be here all day. There is very limited parking along the road to The Braes and for this reason the walk starts at the road end, at Peinachorrain. The subsequent walk back along the road is no hardship at all, but if you want a longer version, then a start from Sligachan is given at the end of the main route description.

Walk back along the road through Peinachorrain, and take the turning onto a minor road on the right Ⓐ. This leads down to overlook Balmeanach Bay, which is an excellent place to watch for birds, especially great northern diver.

When a large open area arrives on the right, with a small hillock in the distance, leave the road Ⓑ and take to the grass, following a narrow trod that leads up to the hillock, which contrives to fashion a lovely surprise view of the bay and across to the adjacent island of Raasay.

Descend from the hillock to a nearby fence corner, and then follow the fence until you can drop down into a narrow ravine, crossed by a narrow plank bridge. Beyond, you now walk firm

> **Tombolo** A tombolo (Italian, from Latin tumulus – mound) is a deposition landform in which an island is attached to the mainland by a narrow piece of land such as a spit or bar. Once attached, the island is then known as a tied island. Tombolos are formed by wave refraction. As waves near an island the shallow water surrounding it slows them down. These waves then refract or 'bend' around the island to the opposite side. The wave pattern created by this water movement causes a convergence of longshore drifting on the opposite side of the island. The waves sweep sediment together from both sides. When enough sediment has built up the beach shoreline will connect with an island and form a tombolo.

machair below a low escarpment, which takes you across a narrow spit of land known as a 'tombolo', linking the former island of An Aird with the mainland of Skye.

Once across to An Aird, you can explore freely. It is worth

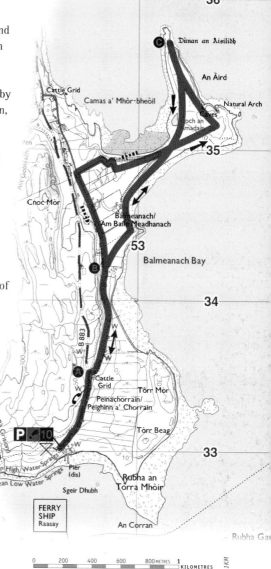

rising onto the modest high point and then following a narrow grassy path northwards, towards the distant profile of Ben Tianavaig. The very northern tip of An Aird is occupied by Dunan an Aislidh ⓒ, a galleried dun, probably Iron Age.

This attractive promontory has small but intricate cliff scenery, and it is worth peering down at it where it is safe to do so. But take care when exploring near the cliff edges, the best section of which is at the far end of the peninsula, where there are a couple of natural arches, sea caves and a blow hole. Return by walking around the edge of Camas a'Mhòr-bheòil, passing close to the shallow Loch an Amadain, and then returning across the tombolo. You can then go back the way you came, or climb above the tombolo and make a little more of Camas a'Mhòr-bheòil before striking across rough grazing to rejoin the road. There turn left, and walk back to Peinachorrain.

Variant start and finish:
You can undertake this walk, starting at Sligachan. A path leaves the main road and follows

Ben Tianavaig from The Braes

surfaced paths through the camp site from the far side of which it sets off alongside Loch Sligachan, crossing a couple of fords and a footbridge, but then taking a clear route parallel with the shoreline. This brings you directly to the road end at Peinachorrain, where you join the above route. This alternative will increase the full walk to 10½ miles, and the height gain to 1,165 feet. ●

SCALE 1:25 000 or 2½ INCHES to 1 MILE 4CM to 1KM

walk 11

Start
Gillen, Waternish

Distance
4 miles (6.5km)

Height gain
770 feet (235m)

Approximate time
2 hours

Route terrain
Forest trails; narrow grassy paths along the top of cliffs

Parking
Single parking space about 270 yds before road end at Gillen, or limited parking at road end: do not obstruct turning circle

OS maps
Landranger 23 (North Skye), Explorer 407 (Skye: Dunvegan)

GPS waypoints
NG 267 595
Ⓐ NG 266 582
Ⓑ NG 287 585
Ⓒ NG 274 595

Beinn an Sguirr and the Waternish Forest

This relaxing walk divides neatly into two halves: the first follows a broad trail through a largely clear-felled area of forest plantation. The second part takes to a narrow grassy path, where heath spotted orchids grow, across the upper escarpment of Beinn an Sguirr high above Loch Snizort. The former is easy, relaxed walking, while the latter, although following a clear grassy path throughout, passes close to spectacular and unstable cliffs. This remote area is inhabited by red deer, while hen harrier, buzzard and golden eagle quarter the heather moors.

Set off past the cottages at Gillen and onto a track through rough grazing to a metal gate. Beyond this, keep ahead, climbing gently, and later ignoring a left turn opposite a quarry (on the right).

Press on for about another 500 yds, and then, at a prominent junction Ⓐ, turn left and walk along a broad track, ascending gradually, and as height is gained, leaving the trees behind. Continue on the main trail, past a signpost pointing out a 'Cliff Walk', and instead keep on to cross a very broad heathery ridge extending north from Beinn Charnach Bheag.

Once across the high point of the ridge, the trail descends gently with fine views over lower woodland to Uig and the hills of Trotternish. Just after the descending trail bends to the right, look for a small cairn on the left Ⓑ, where the ground ahead has been cleared. Here leave the trail by turning onto a narrow trod at the plantation edge, damp in a few places, and gently ascend through banks of heather.

A short distance farther on, at a low turf dyke, you reach the eastern edge of the Beinn an Sguirr escarpment, a surprising and dramatic moment, although the dyke is easily passed by unnoticed. The ongoing path is easy to follow and maintains a comfortable distance, most of the time, from the cliff edges, but does allow tantalising glimpses of the crags.

The path is a pleasure to follow, generally staying away from the trees. In due course you reach a signpost at the other end of the Cliff Walk, and now all that remains is to follow the path out to the track running down to Loch Losait. Some tree felling in the last 100 yds or so means picking your way through, but the forest trail ahead is clear enough, and easy to reach.

The views are spectacular both of the immediate surrounds

and across Loch Snizort to the Ascrib Islands, Uig Bay and the northern hills of Trotternish. Far to the north-west, the islands of the Outer Hebrides – the Western Isles – cruise along the horizon like some great sea monster.

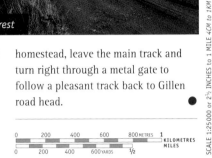

In Waternish Forest

On reaching the forest trail, turn right for a short distance to a junction ●, where the main track swings to the right, down to Loch Losait. At the junction, go left onto a broad track that heads back towards Gillen.

Just after passing a derelict homestead, leave the main track and turn right through a metal gate to follow a pleasant track back to Gillen road head. ●

SCALE 1:25000 or 2½ INCHES to 1 MILE 4CM to 1KM

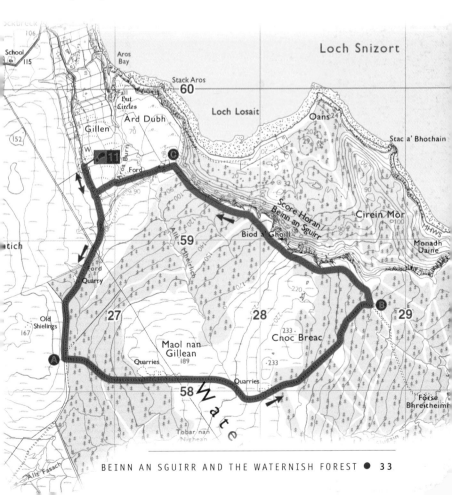

walk 12

Ben Aslak

Start

Bealach Udal, Kylerhea Glen, Strath

Distance

3 miles (5km)

Height gain

1,295 feet (395m)

Approximate time

2½ hours

Route terrain

Rough, largely untracked heather mountain

Parking

Bealach Udal (limited)

OS maps

Landranger 33 (Loch Alsh, Glen Shiel & Loch Hourn), Explorer 412 (Skye: Sleat/Slèite)

GPS waypoints

🖉 NG 755 206

Ⓐ NG 746 200

Ⓑ NG 750 191

The comparatively easy summit of Ben Aslak is best tackled from the high point of the Kylerhea Glen, at the Bealach Udal, just to the east of which there is limited roadside parking. At first, the mountain looks formidable, but the ascent proves easier than expected and is well worth it for the excellent panorama it gives. Few people visit Ben Aslak, which gives this remote summit special appeal; it is perfect for a lazy day.

🖉 The sinuous road that leaves the Broadford road for Kylerhea Glen passes through one of the few truly wild places remaining on Skye. Here, heather moorland, punctuated by rocky outcrops and bogs, plays host to passing buzzards, golden eagles, pipits, skylarks, and not much else. Incredibly, this is the way drovers once brought their cattle from the heart of Skye to swim the sound to Glenelg before an onward march to the lowland trysts, or even to London. Slack water was very much a condition of success, as anyone who has watched the tide rip through here like a river in spate, will know.

Above the kyle, Ben Aslak rises to a modest 2,001 feet in height, and therefore by some standards deemed a mountain – two feet less in height and it would be largely ignored, apart

Ben Aslak

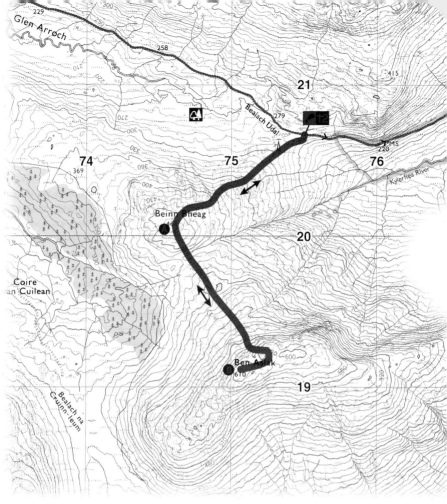

from the fact that these days it ranks as a Marilyn.

The approach from Bealach Udal involves 1,295 feet of ascent, setting off through a metal gate and then following a service track to an aerial compound. Then it tackles a minor top, Beinn Bheag , reached across pathless, heathery, crag-punctuated slopes that in spring and early summer are bright with the yellow eyes of tormentil and the white candy tufts of bog cotton.

Go south and south-east from Beinn Bheag to gain a narrow col, before ascending to a small lochan, and from there pulling up more heathery slopes, aiming slightly closer to south (right) as you approach the summit ●.

Ben Aslak has a surprise lochan, and two summits about 430 yds apart, the higher generally accepted as being that to the west. Both, however, are outstanding viewpoints: the westerly summit for views of the distant Cuillin, while the eastern top gives appetising glimpses into the rough mainland ground of Knoydart beyond Loch Hourn. To the north rise the lumps of Sgurr na Coinnich and Beinn na Caillich.

The only sensible way back is to retrace the outward route. ●

walk (13)

Start
Broadford, Strath

Distance
5¾ miles (9.2km)

Height gain
405 feet (125m)

Approximate time
2½ hours

Route terrain
Road walking; gravel paths; open moorland

Parking
Wooded car park north of cemetery on A87

OS maps
Landranger 32 (South Skye & Cuillin Hills), Explorer 412 (Skye: Sleat/Slèite)

GPS waypoints
NG 624 255
Ⓐ NG 640 236
Ⓑ NG 635 227
Ⓒ NG 627 220
Ⓓ NG 623 226

Coire Chat-achan

Coire Chat-achan is generally thought to mean the 'Corrie of the Wild Cats' in commemoration of the last habitat of wild cats before their extermination in Scotland. But some Gaelic speakers see a reference in the words to a corrie filled with patchy snow. This remote settlement, such as it is, comes in the middle of this walk, which might just as easily begin in Broadford. But by starting a little farther towards Portree and using the remains of the former A87, it is easy enough to lengthen the walk. In spite of its proximity to busy Broadford, this walk passes into a landscape that has a fine sense of remoteness.

Walk out from the parking area and turn left to pass the cemetery. The old road slips away from the modern road beyond the cemetery wall, and this ancient highway, now a lovely path, leads almost all the way to Broadford, flanked in spring and early summer with an abundance of wild flowers.

Beinn na Caillich at Coire Chat-achan

As you approach the outskirts of Broadford, the path rises away from the road to pass through the end of woodland and around a heathery knoll.

Beyond this, the path parallels the road again before finally emerging onto it.

Cross the road (a little to the right), and then turn left onto a road alongside a light industrial estate, with the option of a slight diversion onto a neat little path on the left that runs through a narrow ornamental area.

Keep walking towards Broadford, as far as the bridge ● over Broadford

SCALE 1:25000 or 2½ INCHES to 1 MILE 4CM to 1KM

Beinn na Caillich from Broadford

River. Immediately after the bridge, turn right onto a riverside path, delightful but woefully brief. It leads soon to join the B8083, the Broadford-Elgol road. Turn right and, taking care against approaching traffic once the roadside footpath ends, follow the road as it climbs gently and passes beneath power lines. A short way farther on, you leave the road, by turning left through a gate onto a signed path **B** for Coire Chat-achan.

The path follows the course of an old railway that served the marble quarries at Kilchrist; it makes a delightful trek across the moorland at the entrance to Strath Suardal, but eventually divides. Take the right fork, towards the B-road, and finally cross it close by a grassy mound that bears the name An Sithean **C**. This means 'Fairy Hill', and there are those who are certain that on a quiet night you can sit here and listen to fairy music rising from the mound. Maps, however, show it as a chambered cairn.

Continue past An Sithean, beyond

which the gravel path continues, sweeping round to rejoin Broadford River, finally crossing it at a footbridge **D**. This section of the path is an old highway, first appearing on maps in 1885, but in use for many years before that.

Now walk up towards the farm buildings at Coire Chat-achan. The original house lies in ruins, a Mackinnon home twice visited by Johnson and Boswell in 1773, and a year earlier by Thomas Pennant, who ascended the huge dome of Beinn na Caillich.

Pass around the farm buildings, and up to the modern cottage above. There you reach a surfaced road-end that should now be followed through the linear settlement of Old Corry. Eventually you emerge on the A87. Turn right and walk beside the road towards Broadford for 50m, then cross the road and rejoin the old highway at a fenced opening. Turn left and retrace your outward steps to the start. ●

Heading for Point of Sleat

walk 14

The Quiraing and Meall na Suiramach

Start

Bealach Ollasgairte (not named on maps); the summit of the pass on the Staffin–Uig road, 3 miles (4.75km) west of Staffin, Trotternish

Distance

4 miles (6.5km)

Height gain

1,360 feet (415m)

Approximate time

3 hours

Route terrain

Rough mountain walking; moorland plateau; steep grassy descent

Parking

Bealach Ollasgairte

OS maps

Landranger 23 (North Skye), Explorer 408 (Skye: Trotternish & The Storr)

GPS waypoints

NG 440 679
Ⓐ NG 452 691
Ⓑ NG 448 703
Ⓒ NG 449 694

The crags and pinnacles of the Quiraing are a spectacular feature of the scenery of northern Skye, and most visitors drive over the pass to view them from the road. But, only a minority takes the trouble to explore the lovely path that leads through the landslip beneath its famous features – the Prison, the Needle and the Table. While the walk as far as the Prison is, with a couple of awkward moments, straightforward, it would be foolish to attempt to continue the walk on to Meall na Suiramach in poor visibility, where the ability to navigate competently would be vital.

In high summer you may have to be an early bird to find a place in the lay-by at the top of the pass, though there are more places to park off the road a little closer to Uig.

From the lay-by, cross the road to join the path at a signpost leading towards the enticing pinnacles and rock faces. As you climb, look across the Sound of Raasay to the mountains of the Applecross peninsula – the summit of the pass is at 817 feet so you already enjoy an elevated view of the beautiful landscape. In the light of a fine summer morning, Raasay looks as though it is afloat in a sea of mist. Use your hands when you reach an awkward little gully early in the walk.

Farther on, the path crosses a second stone-filled gully and swings round a buttress. Then the Prison comes into view to the right, an enormous sheer-sided slab of rock, which merits its name. At the end of the ice age, about 11,000 years ago, a bed of solidified lava about 1,000 feet thick, broke away and began to slip towards the sea, creating the weird landscape here. The path bears left to go below the sheer face of the 'Prison', with the 'Needle' to the left. At the col Ⓐ below the Prison there is a cairn that marks where a steep path leads up to the 'Table'. This is badly eroded and does not form part of the present walk, though once, incredibly, cattle were driven up the steep, grassy slope to be concealed in the Table. 'Quiraing' derives from the Norse word meaning 'crooked enclosure', and it is written that 3,000 head of cattle could be concealed here from piratical raiders.

There is no direct way from the Quiraing up onto Meall na Suiramach, and for many walkers, just visiting the Quiraing is sufficient. But, to reach the summit plateau, continue on the

path northwards from Ⓐ, crossing an old fence and passing below an overhanging rock to find a different scene suddenly unveiled. The new, verdant landscape has a small, reed-filled lochan, towered over by vertiginous cliff faces.

Continue past the lochan, walking towards the col and keeping the pinnacles of Leac nan Fionn to the right. Steadily you work a way upwards to reach a ridge linking Meall na Suiramach and Sròn Vourlinn. At NG 450698, a small cairn marks the point where the path divides: the right branch leads to Flodigarry and the Trotternish road; the left is the way to go. A short final pull leads to a fence and step-stile onto the ridge Ⓑ.

Once on the ridge, turn left following a clear path ascending in two distinct phases before reaching the vast summit plateau of Meall na Suiramach at a large cairn Ⓒ. This, however, is not the summit, and to find the trig pillar you must deviate away from the edge. On a clear day, this is not so much a problem;

SCALE 1:25000 or 2½ INCHES to 1 MILE 4CM to 1KM

in mist you will need a compass bearing from the cairn.

Leave the summit trig either by backtracking to the earlier cairn from where you can turn right to parallel the cliff edge, to be guided gradually down sloping moorland to return to Bealach Ollasgairte. Or, you can follow a line of poles from the trig pillar, heading roughly south-west across boggy moor-land. There is a rough path to follow, at least as far as a gate and fence. After that the path is less obvious and the poles steer you away from the direction of Bealach Ollasgairte. The best solution, if using this route, is, as the ground ahead starts to descend, to bear left from the poled route, crossing rough, untracked ground and then finishing steeply down to Bealach Ollasgairte. ●

The way into the Quiraing

Point of Sleat

This short, but not-to-be-underestimated, expedition to the southern end of Skye crams many delights into the journey, especially in spring and early summer when the fields are ablaze with colour; gorse in particular is everywhere during springtime. The objective is the lighthouse at the end of a hummocky peninsula. The approach is along the road from Ardvasar to the Aird of Sleat, where parking is limited.

walk 15

Start
Aird of Sleat, Sleat

Distance
5 miles (8km)

Height gain
1,115 feet (340m)

Approximate time
3 hours

Route terrain
Broad tracks and narrow paths through hummocky terrain; coastal machair; a little rough coast walking

Parking
Limited parking area at start; please do not obstruct farm operations

OS maps
Landranger 32 (South Skye & Cuillin Hills), OS Explorer 412 (Skye: Sleat/Slèite)

GPS waypoints
NG 588 007
NG 576 003
NG 567 004
NM 567 998

The name Sleat (pronounced slate) derives from sleibhte, meaning an extensive tract of moorland, and so it is. This appropriately named thumb of rugged, lochan-laden moorland, wrinkles into a thousand nooks and crannies where Man has battled with the elements to win a living from the unforgiving land. Yet, ironically, Sleat is regarded as 'The Garden of Skye', though not without dissent, for to some extent the gardens are the product of an unhappy time in the island's history, when clan chieftains succumbed to the rule of London, and rode roughshod over the lives and necessities of their tenants. This is nowhere better exemplified than along the tortuous but delightful looping road that visits the isolated communities at Dalavil, Ord, Tokavaig and Tarskavaig, founded at the time of the notorious Highland Clearances when people were forcibly removed from better ground to make way for sheep, and found themselves clinging, almost literally, to the edges of the land.

The concept of an island garden comes, too, from Sleat's more sheltered environment, that allows beech, sycamore and alien conifers to flourish alongside the more natural oak, birch, alder and bramble.

The walk begins through a gate at the road head, and along a broad, rough track that climbs steadily to provide a fine view of the island of Eigg and the shapely Cuillin of Rum. More undulations through a rocky, hummocky landscape climb to the highest point of the track, a small bealach Ⓐ or pass (just south of Sgurran Seilich) from where the onward route wanders downwards towards a distant bay. Initially steep, the descent then leads across a wide hollow through which flows a burn issuing from nearby Loch Aruisg, making a modest splash of a small waterfall and pool before meandering onwards through a rocky gorge.

Final moorland stretch to Point of Sleat

Just before reaching a gate ⑤ leave the main track at a signpost for Point of Sleat and Sandy Bay, climbing briefly to pass beneath the branches of a young oak tree, and then continuing alongside a fence that marks the perimeter of the small settlement here at Acairseid an Rubha.

When the fencing ends, go ahead and soon reach a path junction. If you continue forward at this point you come to a secluded, golden sandy beach, Camas Daraich ⑥. *But if, instead, you branch right, you take to a path easing up on to a hummocky headland with the great lump of Creag Mhor directly behind you. This is the way to the Point of Sleat.*

The ongoing path is continuous, and threads a lovely way across heathery terrain with the Point of Sleat lighthouse coming into view at one point. Gradually you make a way round to a wide break in the rocky outcrops, into which a flight of steps descends. Down these, bear right towards the rocky shoreline, and then swing left to reach a low grassy elevation overlooking another, smaller golden sand beach with the remains of a pier

nearby. From here it is just a few minute's walk by a narrow path onto the sheep-cropped sward that flanks the lighthouse. The view takes in the island of Rum as well as the Scottish mainland around Mallaig and Morar.

This is a beautiful spot, with golden lichen mantling the rocks, and the sound of sea birds ever present. Along the route, although new buildings are being constructed, you may have noticed a number of derelict buildings and lush growths of fuchsia that tell of a more substantial community here than the few crofts that are occupied now. At one time, this tiny fishing harbour supported a population of 80, though the land is intolerant and slow to yield anything other than bog myrtle, heather, ragwort and bog cotton.

The return simply retraces the outward route.

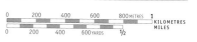

Point of Sleat lighthouse

walk 16

Ben Tianavaig

Start

Camastianavaig, Braes

Distance

5 miles (8km)

Height gain

1,345 feet (410m)

Approximate time

3 hours

Route terrain

Rough, mountain slopes with steep drops to the east; grass and rock outcrops

P Parking

Opposite Tianavaig Bay

OS maps

Landranger 23 (North Skye), Explorer 410 (Skye: Portree & Bracadale)

GPS waypoints

NG 508 389

Ⓐ NG 509 390

Ⓑ NG 516 397

Ⓒ NG 511 410

Ben Tianavaig is a finely sculpted, pyramidal hill, rousing and beautiful, and in view from many parts of the island, yet it is seldom visited by walkers. From the west, the mountain has a neat, symmetrical profile, but from the south, the eastern face is seen to collapse in the landslip manner characteristic of the Trotternish ridge summits. The western aspect is one of bleak peat moorland falling to farmland and rough grazing.

This walk makes a lovely, easy-angled ascent along the cliff edge to the top of Tianavaig, and suggests an alternative descent to the shore and following the coastline back to Tianavaig Bay. Although there are no worthwhile paths, the going is quite easy underfoot and makes use of many sheep tracks, and the whole outing is quite agreeable. Ben Tianavaig is often free of cloud when the Cuillin are shrouded in mist.

From the bay walk north a short distance to the second bend and leave the road at the post box through a fenced break between bungalows (signposted: Creagan) Ⓐ and a group of trees.

Keep on through the break to a boundary fence partially concealed by bracken, beyond which, lies the open moorland. Go left for a short distance above the fence and then start to

Ben Tianavaig from Portree Bay

cross the moor, trending left up a steep heathery slope, and through a low band of rocks. Cross another outburst of rocks and then head for a pronounced lump ahead that proves to be on the cliff edge ●. From here the view is breathtaking, as good as anything on Skye, and proof, if it were needed, that Skye is not all about the Cuillin.

Along the cliff edge, the tussocks of the moor give way to close-cropped turf that eases the steady climb to the trig on the summit ●. *If time is of the essence, or if you want to keep things simple, you will retrace your steps.*

Otherwise, gaze down into a sloping basin below the summit, for this is the way you are going. Begin by going north from the summit, round and down to a grassy bealach on the upper edge of the hollow. Continue round the hollow, keeping to the outer edges to avoid rough and bouldery going in the middle, and pass a pinnacle of rock of the same origin as those found around The Storr and the Quiraing. Here keep on across the hollow. As you reach the other side use more sheep tracks to descend steep grassy slopes to the shore.

A good path now leads you along the shore to Tianavaig Bay. As you pass below Creagan na Sgalain the path scampers beneath a small rock outcrop, after which you can descend to the shoreline and follow it round to your starting point. If the tide plays havoc with this plan, which occasionally it does, go behind the nearby houses to rejoin your outward path.

Camastianavaig, where the ascent begins

Ramasaig, Lorgill and The Hoe

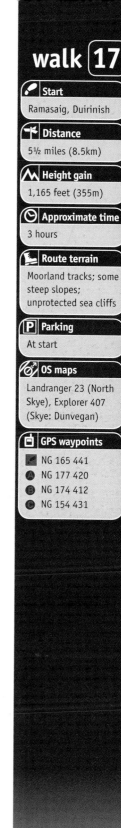

walk 17

Start
Ramasaig, Duirinish

Distance
5½ miles (8.5km)

Height gain
1,165 feet (355m)

Approximate time
3 hours

Route terrain
Moorland tracks; some steep slopes; unprotected sea cliffs

Parking
At start

OS maps
Landranger 23 (North Skye), Explorer 407 (Skye: Dunvegan)

GPS waypoints
NG 165 441
NG 177 420
NG 174 412
NG 154 431

The first part of the walk is easy-going on a good track across moorland, and leads to Lorgill, once a well-populated crofting village sequestered in a remote valley fed by a fine series of waterfalls at its head. The middle section is more energetic and begins with a climb up the steep, grassy slope above Lorgill Bay to the top of the cliff. The way then follows the edge of the cliffs below the Hoe, with magnificent coastal views. From the high point, the final section makes a splendid descent of close-cropped turf flanked to the east by rough moorland, and to the west by dramatic sea cliffs. Because of the risk of startling sheep, especially close to the sea cliffs, it is advised that dogs are held on a lead throughout the walk.

The drive to Ramasaig, in a remote part of Skye, is an enjoyable part of the excursion, with fine coastal views from the road.

Park tidily at Ramasaig, and walk past sheep-pens, cross the bridge spanning Ramasaig Burn, and go through a kissing-gate beside a metal gate. The track passes to the right of a cowshed and soon leaves the Ramasaig pastures. Before long you pass the first of many ruined crofts that dot the landscape, and then cross a ford with a small waterfall just above it. After this the track climbs to cross a low bealach. Pause for a moment here and look back for a glorious view across Moonen Bay to the Neist lighthouse. The cliffs of Waterstein Head, almost 1,000 feet high, are also well seen. A little farther on, the waterfalls descending from Gleann a' Phuill and An Dubh Loch can be seen to the left with the tops of Macleod's Tables beyond.

The track passes through a gate and bends to the left past a long-abandoned croft, with many more now in evidence. Continue following the track down to the substantial ruin of a croft, seen below beside Lorgill River. On reaching the boundary of the croft Ⓐ, turn right to pass through gates, but do not cross the river. Instead, cross a small burn immediately on the right, and then walk alongside a fence until this changes direction. Now keep forward, roughly parallel with the river, heading for Lorgill Bay and following a narrow path for most of the way. The walking is excellent, over springy turf, past the remains of more cottages; whichever way you look the scenery is inspiring, although the story of Lorgill evictions during the Highland Clearances is not a happy one.

You reach Lorgill Bay about an hour after starting from

Ramasaig. From the edge of the Bay you now need to climb the steep grassy slope above. There is a discernible but narrow path slanting left and upwards that begins from the edge of an old croft wall , and this is easier than trying to go straight up. As you climb so the views to the south improve, taking in the imposing Duirinish coastline and eventually bringing into view the sea stacks of Macleod's Maidens.

The sea cliffs of The Hoe are dramatic and sudden, so it is advised not to inspect them too closely. The remains of a fence line act as a guide, with a path running alongside it. Near the high point of the ascent, you intercept a low, turfed dyke running inland, beyond which the climbing soon ends. Anyone wanting to visit the summit of The Hoe can follow the wall upwards, and then cast about to locate the undistinguished summit.

After that, it is all downhill and delightful it is, too. Resist the urge to cut inland, but stay on the lush green grass of the cliff tops, while taking care not to disturb grazing sheep. Sea birds – fulmar, gannets, herring and lesser black-backed gulls – are much in evidence here, and there is always the possibility of spotting seals out at sea or, with good fortune, coastal basking sharks. It was here, at Moonen Bay, that Gavin Maxwell (*of Ring of Bright Water fame*) hunted sharks from his base on the island of Soay, an enterprise explained in his book *Harpoon at a Venture.*

Like Lorgill Bay, the headland of Hoe

The cliffs of The Hoe

Rape 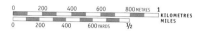 is a lovely place to take a break, with super views across Moonen Bay to the lighthouse at Neist Point. A little closer you can see the splendid cascade of the waterfall where Ramasaig Burn falls to the sea. You are heading towards this, but before reaching it (which is in any case impossible due to barbed wire fencing)

you cross a burn (Abhainn an Lòin Bhàin). Just above is a metal gate, and beyond this you can follow old croft lanes up to the cowshed passed at the start of the walk, and complete the circuit.

SCALE 1:25 000 or 2½ INCHES to 1 MILE 4CM to 1KM

Blà Bheinn

Start
Loch Slapin, Strathaird

Distance
5 miles (8km)

Height gain
3,000 feet (915m)

Approximate time
4 hours

Route terrain
Rugged, rocky mountain terrain throughout

Parking
Near bridge over Allt na Dunaiche, ½ mile (1km) beyond the head of Loch Slapin

OS maps
Landranger 32 (South Skye & Cuillin Hills), Explorer 411 (Skye: Cuillin Hills)

GPS waypoints
NG 561 215
Ⓐ NG 545 216
Ⓑ NG 535 212
Ⓒ NG 534 217

The generosity of Jethro Tull band member Ian Anderson, who owned Blà Bheinn, in agreeing to sell the mountain, meant that it could be bought by the John Muir Trust, an organisation dedicated to safeguarding and protecting Scotland's wilder landscapes. Blà Bheinn is the highest and most southerly of the Cuillin Outliers, and links with the westernmost Red Cuillin in a continuous chain of hills from the southern tip of Strathaird to Sligachan. The customary ascent is by the east ridge, even though, viewed end on, this looks impossibly steep. This is not a walk for other than clear and settled conditions.

The relatively short distance involved in climbing Blà Bheinn is meaningless in terms of how long the ascent will take or the effort required. The walk starts almost at sea level, so it follows that there is a lot of uphill work to be done, much of it on rock.

From the car park provided by the John Muir Trust, either walk out to the road or use a gate towards the rear of the car park to gain a path that will take you down to the road. Turn left for a few strides, and then take to a good path that runs along the northern bank of the Allt na Dunaiche penetrating a wooded gorge, and passing a splash of fine waterfalls en route.

Farther on, cross the Allt na Dunaiche Ⓐ, after which the path starts bearing to the left to a stream at the foot of Coire Uaigneich. A mix of grass and loose stone lies ahead, the ascent more demanding as you climb to pass a large buttress that forms the end of the east ridge.

Allt na Dunaiche The Allt na Dunaiche is variously called the 'Burn of Sorrow', or the 'Burn of Misfortune', a name that alludes to the story of seven girls and a young boy who went to spend the summer in a shieling up above the waterfall, where the burn rises. One day, the girls went out to a wedding, leaving the boy alone. During his lonely vigil, the shieling was entered by seven large cats, which seated themselves by the fire, and talked. The boy watched, spellbound. Then the cats arose, took all the goodness from the butter and the cream, leaving but the appearance of goodness, and vanished. When the girls came home, and the terrified child recounted the story, the girls, seeing what appeared to be butter and cream in plenty, laughed at him, saying it was a dream. Next night, back came the cats, and by dawn all the girls were dead. Later that day, when their mothers came to fetch the butter and cream, as was customary, each, as they entered the shieling and saw the dead girls, cried out 'Airidh mo dunach' (the Shieling of Misfortune).

Sooner than expected, the upper part of the corrie is reached, with Loch Fionna-choire and the satellite, An Stac, off to the east, and the Great Scree Gully directly above 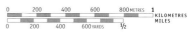. For much of the way the onward route is clear and cairned, though as the upper corrie is ascended, both path and cairns become less apparent.

Now swing to the right and tackle steep grass and rocks to gain the east ridge. There are a number of possible lines, all eventually achieving the broad crest of the ridge. Once this is gained, the onward route is much more evident, and ascends through stony grooves and up rocky buttresses to a spectacular view of Clach Glas between the walls of an intervening gully 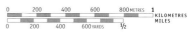.

SCALE 1:25 000 or 2½ INCHES to 1 MILE 4CM to 1KM

0	200	400	600	800 METRES	1
					KILOMETRES
					MILES
0	200	400	600 YARDS	½	

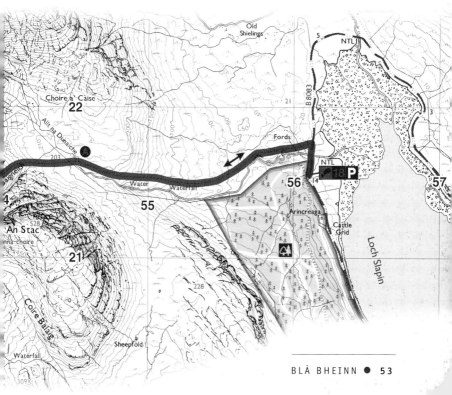

Continue ascending, with improving views of Clach Glas, before progressing upwards on a clearly trodden path with a little easy scrambling en route (although most of this can be avoided), before finally emerging on the summit shoulder, with only a short, easy walk remaining up to the trig point and cairn. The view of the Cuillin that greets the last few strides is breathtaking and sudden, and matched only by that of the great gullies sweeping down into Glen Sligachan.

To return, retrace the ascent, though this may prove difficult and potentially dangerous in misty conditions. If mists do suddenly appear, head for the col between the two summits and descend the Great Scree Gully, with the greatest care.

Heading to Blà Bheinn

The Storr

The Storr (2,359 feet) is the highest summit along the Trotternish ridge, and the place where the dramatic land-slipped scenery for which the ridge is famous, begins. This fairly straightforward way onto The Storr yields to a steady, plodding approach, which in spite of crossing often wet moorland, is entertaining in an introspective kind of way. Certainly, once you reach the ridge, a whole new perspective opens up across the central and western parts of Skye.

walk 19

Start
Small parking area near waterfall on A855, Trotternish

Distance
6 miles (9.5km)

Height gain
2,130 feet (650m)

Approximate time
4 hours

Route terrain
Boggy moorland; untracked grassy, mountain upland

P Parking
At start (limited)

OS maps
Landranger 23 (North Skye), Explorer 408 (Skye: Trotternish & The Storr)

GPS waypoints
NG 495 510
NG 485 513
NG 489 532

There is no significant path from the parking area at the start; just a self-belief (or hope) that you can cross the moorland to the west without too much difficulty, as, to be fair, is usually the case.

Go through the gate at the start, and take a wet path that angles away to the right from below the nearby waterfall. After an initial rise, swing more to the left and just stride out across the moor, aiming to the right of Bealach Mòr on the skyline.

As you progress onto the moor, the ground rises more noticeably. Ahead, you can pick out a slanting rake rising right to left up to the bealach, and you should head for this, and follow it to the col. Along the way there are inspiring views of shapely Ben Dearg off to the left (south-west). It is a tempting mountain, but one that can be left for another day as its conquest is not straightforward.

The early part of the walk to The Storr

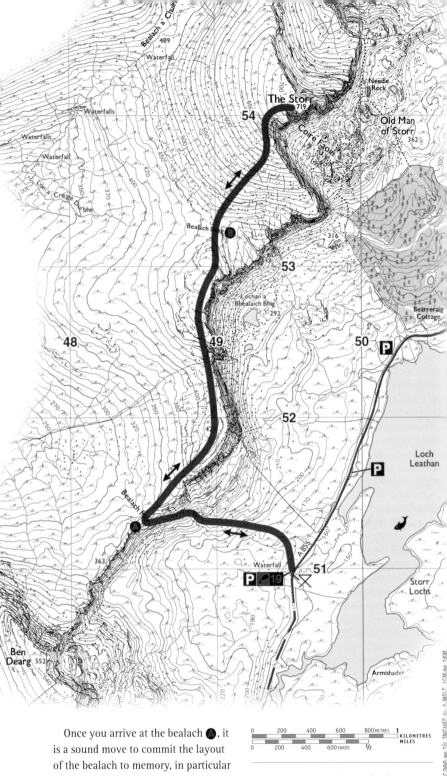

Once you arrive at the bealach Ⓐ, it is a sound move to commit the layout of the bealach to memory, in particular a moderate-sized rock with a small cairn on top of it, as this marks the start of the descent on the way back.

The view from the bealach is

Storr and the Old Man of Storr from Loch Fada

fascinating; to the west lies an area of Skye seldom if ever visited by walkers, and drained by the rivers Haultin and

The starting point for the walk to The Storr

Romesdal and the tributary Lòn Mòr. It offers excellent exploration for anyone willing to cast pathways adrift and indulge in careful navigation.

A line of ancient fence stanchions runs across Bealach Mòr, and onward towards The Storr. *You can follow this, although stray bits of wire are a trip hazard, and the accompanying path passes quite close to minor cliff edges.* It is safer to take to the high ground, keeping the fenceline in sight, and heading roughly northwards over two minor bumps to reach Bealach Beag ●.

Beyond, all that remains is the pull up long, grassy slopes to the summit. Choose your own line, but opt for one that fairly closely follows the cliff edges, which will reward with glimpses down into Coire Faoin and the Storr Sanctuary.

Return the way you came, and enjoy expansive views as good as any on Skye.   ●

Ruined church of Cill
Chriosd, Strath Suardal

Rubh' an Dùnain

This linear coastal walk is a delight, leading into a mildly tormented landscape of lava flows that once echoed to the sounds of MacAskill life. The walk is perfectly straightforward, but demands rather more energy than it might seem at first sight. Rubh' an Dùnain has a keen aura of mystery and romance, a sheltered and secluded location, with an ancient fort, deserted settlement and ancient chambered cairn.

walk 20

Start
Glen Brittle, Cuillin, Minginish

Distance
7¼ miles (11.6km)

Height gain
1,180 feet (360m)

Approximate time
5 hours

Route terrain
Rough tracks; undulating moorland dotted with craggy outcrops

Parking
At the end of the road down to the Glen Brittle camping site; please park considerately

OS maps
Landranger 32 (South Skye & Cuillin Hills), Explorer 411 (Skye: Cuillin Hills)

GPS waypoints
NG 409 206
Ⓐ NG 415 191
Ⓑ NG 402 172
Ⓒ NG 393 163
Ⓓ NG 395 170

Many walkers visit Rubh' an Dùnain when the higher fare of the Cuillin is shrouded in mist. Yet there is no grander vision of the Cuillin than that seen on the return journey. For this reason, choose a clear day, and you will see the crags and gullies of the Cuillin to great effect. If that fails, think of Rubh' an Dùnain as a place where you can go to relax, and spend some time in peaceful isolation. Historically, the area offers a rare opportunity to view a group of structures covering more than 4,000 years of Skye's history, from the Neolithic age through to the 18th century

From the end of the road, walk towards the campsite and go on to pass the toilet block. Through a kissing-gate at the rear of the building take the rough, ascending path that climbs to a broad track that will be seen to run out along the Rubh' an Dùnain peninsula. The route, never in doubt, follows the eastern shore of Loch Brittle along the edge of cliffs, although these are barely noticeable in the early stages of the walk. Out to sea, Canna is the closest of the offshore islands at this point.

You need to cross the Allt Coire Làgan Ⓐ about 1 mile from the start and this is rarely a problem, but if the burn is in spate you may have to divert downstream to cross it by a bridge just below the main track. In any case, it is worth pausing here for a moment as there are lovely waterfalls that provide foregrounds for spectacular views of the Cuillin.

The onward-leading path skirts the upthrust of Creag Mhòr, but those who want to visit this modest high point will find a convenient path leading upwards towards higher ground. The summit provides a wonderful panorama of Hebridean islands. Canna, Rum and Eigg lie close at hand to the south while South Uist and Barra can be seen to the west.

walk 21

Marsco

Start
Sligachan

Distance
7½ miles (12km)

Height gain
2,510 feet (765m)

Approximate time
5 hours

Route terrain
Rough heather moorland; steep mountain slopes, mainly grass and rock outcrops

Parking
At various locations around Sligachan

OS maps
Landranger 32 (South Skye & Cuillin Hills), Explorer 411 (Skye: Cuillin Hills)

GPS waypoints
NG 486 298
Ⓐ NG 495 272
Ⓑ NG 513 260
Ⓒ NG 511 249

The distinctive profile of Marsco when viewed from Sligachan is one of the finest sights among the high mountains of Skye; its very independence from other summits gives its bold, sweeping, pyramidal lines great appeal. There are no special difficulties on this ascent, but it is not for novices: expect rough and strenuous walking once you reach the base of the mountain. Unlike neighbouring summits, very little scree is encountered on Marsco. This is not a summit to attempt in less than good visibility.

 Start from the old bridge at Sligachan, just beyond which a path for Loch Coruisk and Kilmarie starts at a gate. The clear, often stony, path moves on across a long moorland stretch dominated by the dark gaze of the Black Cuillin. The glen route encounters numerous feeder burns before reaching the rather more substantial Allt na Measarroch about 2 miles into the glen. This is the point of departure for Marsco.

Just before the burn and an old fenceline, there is a path junction Ⓐ marked by a low cairn on the left. Branch left here onto a narrow path through heather, heading up alongside the burn, and climbing steadily into the Coire Dubh Measarroch. The path is not always clear, but if lost it is easy enough to follow the course of the burn, climbing all the time to reach the boggy pass, Màm a'Phobuill Ⓑ.

> **A royal route** Although shown on maps as Màm a' Phobuill, the Pass of the People, there is a local tradition that this broad bealach is known as The Prince's Pass, Màm a' Phrionnsa, adding weight to the contested theory that the route taken by Bonnie Prince Charlie lay through the glen between Marsco and Beinn Dearg Mheadhonach and into Coire nam Bruadaran, the Corrie of Dreams.

Above the pass, a lovely corrie scoops into the flesh of Marsco. This is Coire nan Laogh, the Corrie of the Calves, and the key to the continuation of the route, and for that matter the start of the return, as the route follows one arm of the corrie going up and the other coming down. If the prospect of the steep slope above you when viewed from Màm a' Phobuill is too daunting, then simply retreat; it is a demanding haul up to

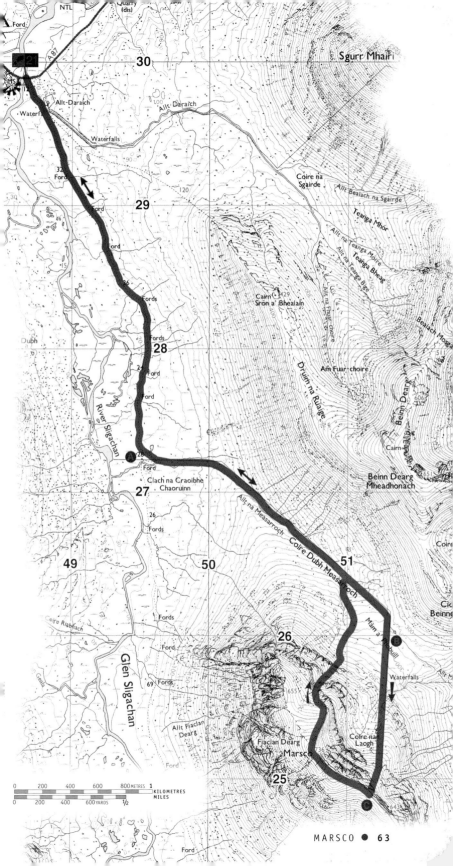

Marsco seen from the top of Blà Bheinn

the summit, followed by a descent that will test the strongest knees.

To gain the upward, easterly edge of Coire nan Laogh, cross the Allt Màm a' Phobuill, which issues from the corrie and ends in a waterfall in a deep ravine. Once across the burn, follow a line of old fence posts up the side of the corrie. The ascent is steep and tiring, but not difficult and leads to the south-east ridge of Marsco at a slight dip ⬤. From here the way to the summit lies up a narrow ridge to the right, the highest point crowned by a modest cairn. Not surprisingly this is a fabulous viewpoint with the Black Cuillin so close, but the bulk of Blà Bheinn and Garbh-bheinn are just as impressive.

To return, either retrace your upward steps, or set off northwards and then turn north-east down the more northerly arm of the Coire nan Laogh. This is a steeper and rougher option than the way up, especially half-way down, but finally it pans out into a steep rake of grass that in turn feeds into easier slopes above Màm a' Phobuill. Once this bealach is regained, it is simply a question of retreating by the outward route down the Allt na Measarroch to the main path through Glen Sligachan. Having rejoined the glen route, turn right to return to Sligachan. ⬤

Glen Brittle Forest

Unlike many forest walks, this spin around Glen Brittle Forest provides good views, especially of Loch Eynort and the Cuillin summits above Coire a'Ghreadaidh and Coire na Creiche. This is a fine excursion for a 'rest' day, one on which you can study the many and varied trees in the forest – sitka spruce, Corsican pine, Japanese larch, Austrian pine, goat willow, alder and Douglas fir.

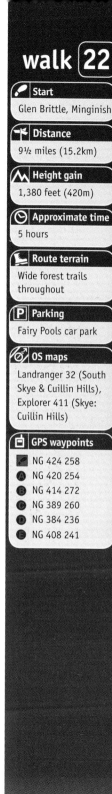

walk 22

Start
Glen Brittle, Minginish

Distance
9½ miles (15.2km)

Height gain
1,380 feet (420m)

Approximate time
5 hours

Route terrain
Wide forest trails throughout

Parking
Fairy Pools car park

OS maps
Landranger 32 (South Skye & Cuillin Hills), Explorer 411 (Skye: Cuillin Hills)

GPS waypoints
NG 424 258
Ⓐ NG 420 254
Ⓑ NG 414 272
Ⓒ NG 389 260
Ⓓ NG 384 236
Ⓔ NG 408 241

A number of thoughtfully positioned picnic tables, all with fine views, are an added attraction, and mean that you can saunter round enjoying the views from many vantage points. The sameness of the terrain – forest, trails and views – suggests that this walk is plain and uninteresting. But there is much of interest, not least with every change of direction when you come to see familiar mountain and valley faces from different angles. Forest clearance has done much to enhance the views, which maintain interest throughout the walk.

From the parking area, pass through a nearby gate to gain a gently rising track. At a junction Ⓐ, turn sharply to the right to begin a long and steadily rising climb along the edge of the forest. When you intercept another track Ⓑ, turn left, and now stay on a twisting trail for over two miles, with improving snapshots of Glen Eynort, the double-topped Cnoc Scarall, Biod Mór across the glen, and later Loch Eynort.

On reaching a junction (NG 389267), where a path (the Cuckoo Road) descends to the right towards Glen Eynort, ignore it and bear left, climbing to another junction at a U-bend Ⓒ at the head of a wooded ravine. Go right, walking around the ravine and then swing left above the end of Loch Eynort, shortly reaching the first picnic table (NG 382254), which offers a lovely view out to sea. Beyond the picnic table you pursue a splendid terraced trail high above Loch Eynort, with ever-expanding views seawards.

Gradually you leave Loch Eynort behind and amble on past an area that has been clear felled, and soon arrive at a T-junction Ⓓ. Turn left and, a few strides farther on, cross the infant Allt Dabhoch, amid a rash of tree remains. Ignore the turning on the right to Kraiknish that soon follows.

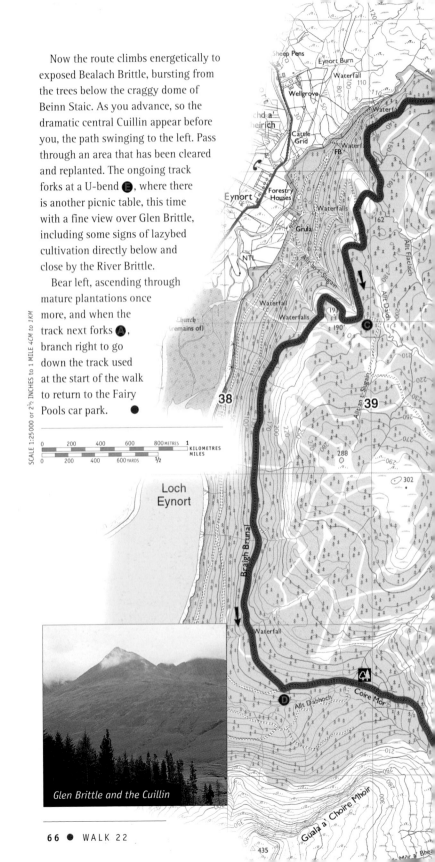

Now the route climbs energetically to exposed Bealach Brittle, bursting from the trees below the craggy dome of Beinn Staic. As you advance, so the dramatic central Cuillin appear before you, the path swinging to the left. Pass through an area that has been cleared and replanted. The ongoing track forks at a U-bend ●, where there is another picnic table, this time with a fine view over Glen Brittle, including some signs of lazybed cultivation directly below and close by the River Brittle.

Bear left, ascending through mature plantations once more, and when the track next forks ●, branch right to go down the track used at the start of the walk to return to the Fairy Pools car park. ●

SCALE 1:25 000 or 2½ INCHES to 1 MILE 4CM to 1KM

Glen Brittle and the Cuillin

walk 23

Start
Orbost, Duirinish

Distance
10 miles (16km)

Height gain
1,770 feet (540m)

Approximate time
5½ hours

Route terrain
Moorland; coastal margins, sometimes rocky; steep cliffs; cleared forest

Parking
Limited at start

OS maps
Landranger 23 (North Skye), Explorer 407 (Skye: Dunvegan)

GPS waypoints
NG 257 431
NG 251 422
NG 249 409
NG 250 398
NG 247 362

Idrigill Point and MacLeod's Maidens

MacLeod's Maidens are the finest sea stacks on Skye, lying at the southernmost point of the Duirinish peninsula, off Idrigill Point. The highest of the stacks is the tallest on Skye, rising to more than 200 feet (65m). This walk, which follows a delightful route along the western side of Loch Bracadale, leads to a viewpoint on the nearby cliff, overlooking the stacks. It is undoubtedly among the finest coastal walks on the island, and follows a good path throughout, although you have to leave it to get a view of the stacks.

Go past Orbost Farm and Orbost House, and down a rough farm track to reach Loch Bharcasaig, its pebbly beach framed on the left by the low headland of Meall Greepa and on the right by the partially wooded slopes of Cnoc na Pairce, which are steadily being cleared.

Cross the Abhainn Bharcasaig at the far side of the bay to continue along a broad track rising steadily into the older part of the forest. The track through this section is pleasant, felling and storm damage having significantly reduced the blanket cover of trees. Now there are views across the bay, and glimpses of Beinn na Boineid inland, which do much to draw you on. Forest Enterprise has created a welcome variety of green foliage, replacing conifers with broad-leaved trees, notably

MacLeod's Maidens

alongside the burns and at the forest boundaries. Further improvement has come in the form of clear felling, which has reduced the amount of time spent among trees.

Shortly after leaving the forest you traverse a large cleared area, which now provides spacious views across Loch Bracadale to the Cuillin. The track passes through a wall 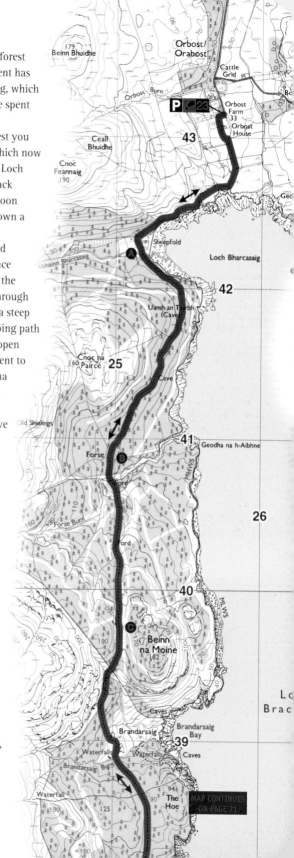, and soon reaches Forse Burn tumbling down a rocky gully. It is usually easy enough to ford the burn, beyond which you encounter a deer fence and gate. Just beyond the gate, the path forks. Bear right, briefly through bracken and heather to ascend a steep bank on a rocky path. The ongoing path shortly wanders across a large open area, and leads to a gradual ascent to the bealach ● between Beinn na Boineid and Beinn na Moine. A splendid view now opens up across the mountain corrie above Brandarsaig Bay.

Descend from the bealach across heathery slopes, and soon pass through three deer fence/gates in fairly quick succession. At the third gate you enter Rebel's Wood, an area of new planting by Future Forests dedicated in the living memory of Joe Strummer (1952-2002), lead singer and rhythm guitarist of the punk rock band, The Clash.

After the gate the path crosses the corrie to reach a convenient commemorative bench above the abandoned crofts of Brandarsaig, a perfect spot for a breather. The view embraces nearby Harlosh Island, the Harlosh peninsula and a skyline extending from the Trotternish ridge to the left and

Glamaig, the first of the Red Cuillin to the right. A nearby burn gully is lined with the ubiquitous rowan and a couple of aspen.

Across the corrie the track climbs again onto heather moorland before descending to cross Idrigill Burn, directly below Ben Idrigill. After the

Idrigill Point

burn crossing, a lovely green track leads on between heathery knolls and brackeny slopes as you approach the inlet of Camas na h-Uamha.

The walk now turns inland through Glac Ghealaridh, a pleasant heather carpet between low hills. Once beyond the two small hills – Steineval and Ard Beag – the path passes through a deer fence and gradually bears left to another close by croft ruins as it steers south-west towards Idrigill Point.

The on-going path rounds the bay, Inbhir a'Ghàrraidh, but well before this you should abandon it and head across short turf for the cliff tops, exploring with care, and following the line of cliffs west for a fine view of the Maidens ●. *Take great care at the cliff edges.*

Return, leisurely, by your outward route. ●

200 400 600 800 METRES 1 KILOMETRES MILES
200 400 600 YARDS ½

MacLeod's Maidens

Legend relates that the MacLeod's Maidens were so named when the wife and two daughters of the Fourth Chief of the Clan MacLeod perished there in a boat that had drifted before a strong westerly wind across the Minch from Harris, to be pounded to pieces on the Maidens.

The largest of the Maidens is said to be not unlike statues of a seated Queen Victoria when seen from the sea. She is the Mother, and is said to be constantly weaving. Walter Scott called the Maidens the 'Choosers of the Slain' in an allusion to the last appearance of the Valkyries over this part of Skye as they fled before the coming Christianity. It was the custom of the Valkyries to weave a web of death before a battle, and then choose the best and bravest of the slain and lead them to Valhalla.

The Maidens, too, were notorious wreckers of ships, some say aided by the practice of smuggler Campbell of Ensor, who used the Black Skerries at the Maidens' feet to position false lights.

walk 25

Bruach na Frithe

Start

Sligachan

Distance

8¼ miles (13.2km)

Height gain

3,050 feet (930m)

Approximate time

6 hours

Route terrain

Rough moorland; rugged, high mountain corrie

P Parking

Limited at start, alongside the Dunvegan road

OS maps

Landranger 32 (South Skye & Cuillin Hills), Explorer 411 (Skye: Cuillin Hills)

GPS waypoints

NG 479 297
NG 455 278
NG 459 265
NG 463 254

Walkers wanting for the first time to get a flavour of the Cuillin, will find Bruach na Frithe ideal for the purpose. The summit, which lies only a short distance from rather more difficult ascents on Am Bhasteir and Sgurr nan Gillean, is regarded as 'easy', but only in the context of Britain's most complex and demanding range of mountains. The only approach that does not involve scrambling is that through Fionn Choire, and even this is a demanding and energetic exercise, and potentially confusing in poor visibility. The first recorded ascent was in 1845, by Professor James Forbes and Duncan MacIntyre.

Though less obviously a dramatic corrie than others crammed beneath the black crags of the Cuillin, the hummocky expanse of Coire na Circe spreads about the Allt Dearg Mór, and is a traditional cross-country route between Sligachan and Glen Brittle, reached across the Bealach a' Mhaim.

Leave the roadside lay-by, and turn onto a broad track (signposted: 'Footpath to Glen Brittle') that leads to Allt Dearg House. As the house is approached, leave the track and move right, onto a peaty path that can be messy after rain. This stretch, however, is soon passed, and the on-going path improves with height, becoming a stony path on which good progress is made.

The walk beside the Allt Dearg Mór is enlivened by chattering cascades and bright-eyed pools, and is a delight. In poor weather, this riparian ramble, as far as Bealach a'Mhaim, can make a suitable walk in itself.

About ½ mile before the Bealach a' Mhaim, at a small cairn, the path forks Ⓐ. Here, leave the main path, and go left shortly to cross the burn (Allt Dearg Mór) at an easy ford. Beyond this, a clear path ascends steadily, parallel with the Allt an Fhionn-choire, and heading for Fionn Choire. On reaching the corrie rim, the burn appears ahead in a deep gully, easily crossed to enter the corrie above Ⓑ.

The onward path is now cairned, but not abundantly so. The mountain pass, Bealach nan Lice, lies at the head of the corrie, to the left, with a stony path rising to it. Head in this direction. If going no farther than the corrie there is quite a sizeable arena to explore in which a few small lochans repose. This can be

Sgurr nan Gillean from Bruach na Frithe

quite a suntrap on a hot day, so be sure to carry plenty of liquid.

To reach the bealach, continue with the path, tending to the left, and rising to meet a bouldery, and then scree, path as the headwall of the corrie is approached. Paths, from Sgurr a' Bhasteir, arrive from the left, joining with the Fionn Choire path just below the bealach Ⓒ. The 'surprise' view of Lota Corrie from the bealach is outstanding. Sgurr a'Fionn Choire stands immediately to the west of the Bealach nan Lice, and is another splendid viewpoint, but its ascent is a scramble of about 150 feet, not a walk.

At the Bealach nan Lice, traverse right, below Sgurr a'Fionn Choire (on the Fionn Choire side), on a good path (take the higher of the two on offer) that leads to a shallow bealach between Sgurr a' Fionn Choire and Bruach na Frithe, where the rest of the main ridge springs into view. The ensuing East Ridge of Bruach na Frithe is no more than a moderate walk, with a little optional scrambling en route. The view from the summit – the only Cuillin summit with a triangulation pillar – is one of the Cuillin's finest.

The only return route, is that by which the ascent was made. ●

Glen Sligachan

This magnificent and dramatic glen, the finest on Skye, forms the eastern boundary of Minginish, separating the Cuillin from Strathaird. For walkers it is an ideal place to become familiar with Skye terrain, and the sort of problems it presents. The walk from Sligachan to Camasunary is for anyone a superb undertaking, even on a rainy day. But the distances through the glen should not be underestimated, and if there has been prolonged rain, then the going at the numerous burn crossings can be very trying. Anyone in search of a long low-level walk will find nothing better on Skye. The route continues from Camasunary by climbing over the southerly ridge that spills from Blà Bheinn to the road at Kilmarie.

Start	Sligachan
Finish	Kilmarie, Strathaird
Distance	10¼ miles (16.5km)
Height gain	1,445 feet (440m)
Approximate time	6 hours
Route terrain	Rough mountain glen, with many burn crossings; good path throughout
Parking	At start
OS maps	Landranger 32 (South Skye & Cuillin Hills), Explorer 411 (Skye: Cuillin Hills)
GPS waypoints	NG 486 298 Ⓐ NG 495 271 Ⓑ NG 501 242 Ⓒ NG 502 240 Ⓓ NG 545 172

Progress through Glen Sligachan is invariably affected by the recent weather. After heavy or sustained rain, expect to ford many of the burns (or make tiring detours) and to plod through what seems like never-ending bog. But that gives completely the wrong impression, because in good conditions, it is so remarkably different.

The walking ranks as magnificent in any conditions. Walkers unable to arrange pickups or to complete the whole walk should consider going as far as the Lochan Dubha, near the entrance to Harta Corrie. This in itself is an excellent walk, and presents both Sgurr nan Gillean and Marsco from unfamiliar angles, as well as giving an insight into the depths of Harta Corrie and across to the heights of the Cuillin.

Close by the old bridge at Sligachan, take the signposted path through a gate for Loch Coruisk. The path moves on in stages: first a long moorland stretch as the route heads towards shapely Marsco, then a stretch dominated by Sgurr nan Gillean. A narrowing follows, as the glen passes the Lochan Dubha and heads for Blà Bheinn before bursting out into the loveliness that is Camasunary. The final stage is eastwards over the low bealach of Am Màm to the main road at Kilmarie.

The way encounters numerous feeder burns before reaching the rather more substantial Allt na Measarroch. Cross the burn, almost always a wet proposition, and continue to a prominent heather-topped boulder, Clach na Craoibhe Chaoruinn Ⓐ.

More pleasant walking beneath the great slopes of Marsco ensues, climbing gently to a high point Ⓑ overlooking the Lochan Dubha from where there is a fine view through Harta

Corrie to the dark central peaks of the Black Cuillin – Sgurr Alasdair, Sgurr Mhic Choinnich and Sgurr Dearg and its Inaccessible Pinnacle.

At the entrance to the corrie stands a shrub-encrusted boulder, the Bloody Stone, which features among the many tales of the clashes between the MacDonalds and the MacLeods.

SCALE 1:25000 or 2½ INCHES to 1 MILE 4CM to 1KM

The Bloody Stone In 1395 the MacDonalds sent a force of galleys to invade Skye. They landed at Loch Eynort and rapidly progressed east towards Sligachan, where they met a formidable response from the MacLeods, and a furious battle ensued during which the invaders were thrown into confusion, which soon became a rout. The MacLeods ruthlessly pursued them back to Loch Eynort where, with cruel fate, the MacAskills had seized their galleys and moored them off shore. It is said that not one of the invaders survived, and that the heads of the slain were collected, numbered and sent to Dunvegan as trophies to be retained in the custody of the warden of Dunvegan Castle. It was at Creag an Fheannaidh, The Rock of the Flaying, now known as the Bloody Stone, that the spoils of battle were divided.

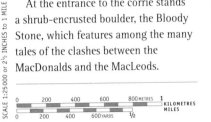

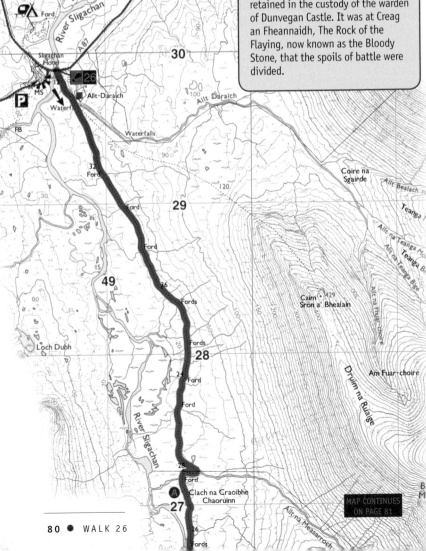

MAP CONTINUES ON PAGE 81

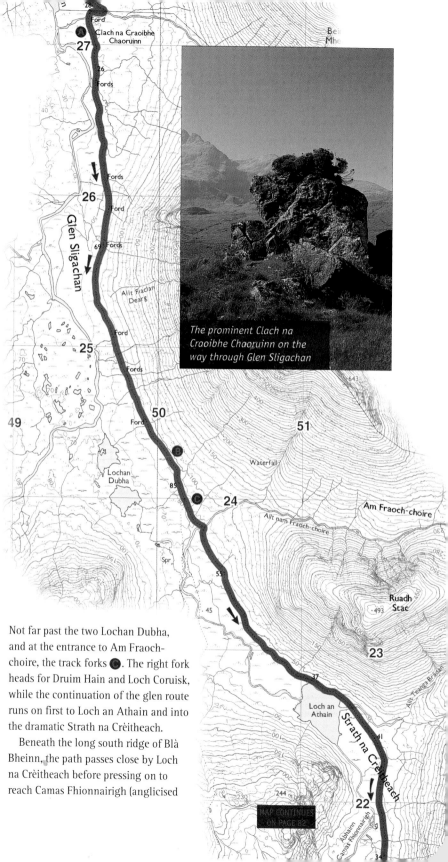

The prominent Clach na Craoibhe Chaoruinn on the way through Glen Sligachan

Not far past the two Lochan Dubha, and at the entrance to Am Fraoch-choire, the track forks **C**. The right fork heads for Druim Hain and Loch Coruisk, while the continuation of the glen route runs on first to Loch an Athain and into the dramatic Strath na Crèitheach.

Beneath the long south ridge of Blà Bheinn, the path passes close by Loch na Crèitheach before pressing on to reach Camas Fhionnairigh (anglicised

MAP CONTINUES ON PAGE 82

to Camasunary), one of the most enchanting places on the entire island, and an entirely relaxing place to be. Here a wide sandy beach runs into a bright green sward of meadow on which two buildings, one a bothy, the other private, provide a stark contrast to the background darkness of Sgurr na Stri and Blà Bheinn. Camasunary is a place destined to capture hours of your time, tranquil and relaxing.

The conclusion of the walk lies to the east, via a broad track slanting up and across the hillside to a low bealach, Am Màm. It is clear and easy to follow, rough underfoot but a broad track all the way, and leads out to the Elgol-Broadford road at Kilmarie Ⓓ. ●

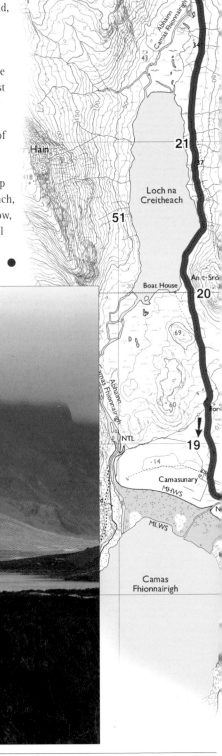

Loch an Athain

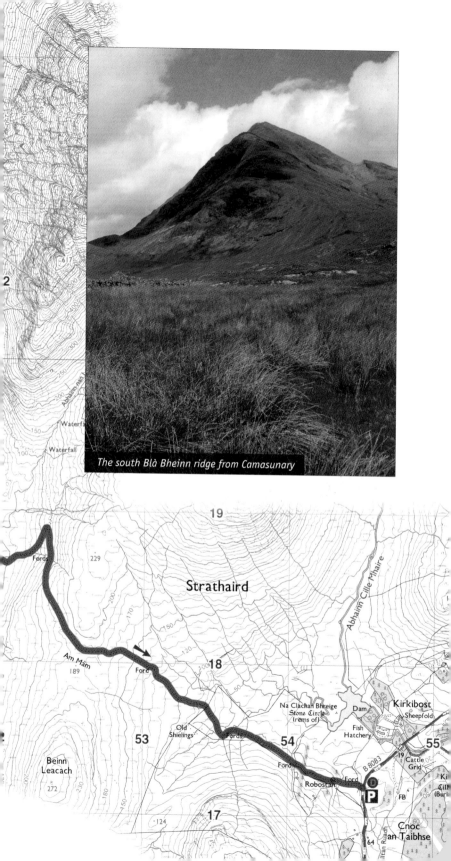

The south Blà Bheinn ridge from Camasunary

walk `27`

Start

Head of Loch Slapin, near Abhainn an t-Sratha Mhòir

Distance

11 miles (17.5km)

Height gain

1,265 feet (385m)

Approximate time

6½ hours

Route terrain

Rugged mountain glens with numerous burn crossings

Parking

At start

OS maps

Landranger 32 (South Skye & Cuillin Hills), Explorer 411 (Skye: Cuillin Hills)

GPS waypoints

NG 565 224
NG 562 251
NG 566 265
NG 593 265

Srath Mòr and Srath Beag

Despite both running north–south, the two glens of Srath Mòr and Srath Beag, typical Highland glens, contrive to link the east and west coast of Skye. Between them they enclose a minor summit, Beinn na Crò, an optional add-on for the energetic. This is the route (in part) taken by Bonnie Prince Charlie as he journeyed across Skye in 1746, bound for the safety of France. In times of spate it is difficult if not impossible to cross the Abhainn an t-Sratha Mhòir when the path switches sides near the lochan.

From the road bridge spanning the Abhainn an t-Sratha Mhóir set off along a clear, stony track, soon passing Clach Oscar (Oscar's Stone), a large split boulder tossed here by Oscar, son of Ossian, one of the legendary Fiennes, or Fianna, in a moment of merriment. The track soon reaches the shores of Loch na Sguabaidh, where, after prolonged rain, it can often be flooded.

> **Loch na Sguabaidh**   Loch na Sguabaidh used to be inhabited by a waterhorse that preyed upon any pretty girl who wandered within his reach. Plain lassies were thought to be safe enough; indeed, to have been captured by the waterhorse and to have escaped was to assure a reputation as a beauty. The waterhorse's taste for mischief, however, eventually led to his demise, as, en route to Loch na Crèitheach, the beast was killed by MacKinnon of Strath in Bealach na Beiste (the Pass of the Beast).

Beyond the loch the path remains clear but is in poor condition, though it never climbs higher than 55 feet. As you approach Lochan Stratha Mhòir Ⓐ the path switches sides of the glen, crossing the Abhainn an t-Sratha Mhòir. Now the path drops gently as it heads for Luib, a former crofting hamlet, now with a small crofting museum. Approaching Luib, the path forks Ⓑ. Branch right, taking the most direct route to the village.

On reaching the village road, go immediately right, but as the road bends left, leave it at a gate for the old Broadford-Portree road, which now climbs across the southern slopes of Am Meall, north of Loch nam Madadh Uisge, and provides much improved going as far as the Allt Strollamus Ⓒ. Please ensure as you walk this old highway, flanked by rough grazing for

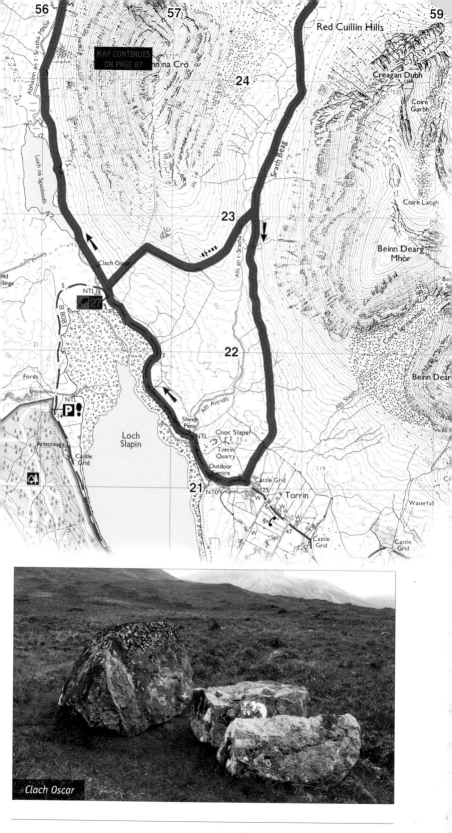

Clach Oscar

Loch na Sguabaidh, Srath Mòr

sheep, that all gates are left as you found them.

Leave the old road above the scattered houses that are Strollamus, but do not cross the river, leaving the track at a bridge and keeping instead to its east bank, along a path that climbs into the narrows of An Slugan. Rather more ascent is ahead, rising to about 625 feet to reach a wide, grassy bealach where the path switches sides as in Srath Mòr.

Now press on down Srath Beag, high above the true left bank of Allt an t-Sratha Bhig, to join a broad track just before you reach the road at Torrin, opposite a welcome café. Turn right and stroll along the road back to the start, while keeping an eye open for birdlife on the loch.

The finish can be shortened by recrossing the Allt an t-Sratha Bhig towards the southern end of Srath Beag, and climbing across rough ground to intercept the boundary of a large fenced enclosure and follow this back to return to the start.

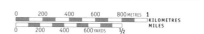

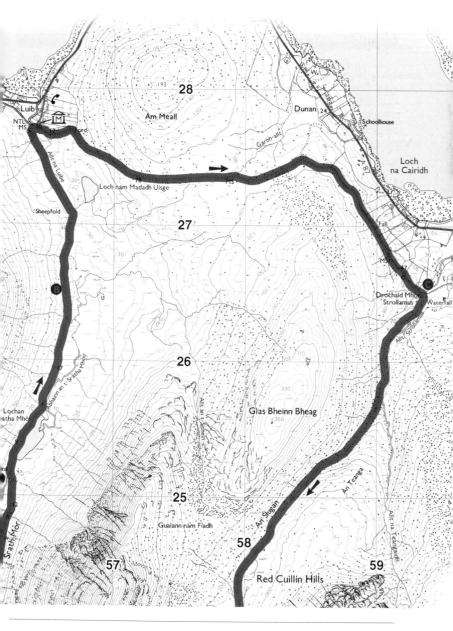

Loch Coruisk, and the point of access to the cave in which Prince Charles Edward Stuart (Bonnie Prince Charlie) spent his last night on Skye.

As you descend into Elgol, branch left onto the narrow road for Glasnakille. *(You can, of course, simply turn left on meeting the main road and follow it back to Kilmarie.)*

The road walking to Glasnakille is an easy interlude, and leads through a twisted landscape to a T-junction by a telephone box . Turn left here, the road continuing as far as a croft. Now the route continues as a beautiful birch-fringed track descending to cross a stream and entering woodland. On leaving the woodland, you soon reach another surfaced lane, which climbs steadily, but, when there is a brief respite from the ascent and it makes a sweeping left-hand turn, take the track that goes ahead to a white cottage.

About 50 yds before the cottage, take a faint track to the right, which descends and follows the shoreline of the loch. This passes the site of a long-abandoned croft to reach a gate in a deer fence. Now follow the track out past an old graveyard described by Otta Swire as: '... strange, unexpected, and rather desolate, with the pebbles of the seashore reaching to its gates. It has been planted with yew and cypress; purple flags and red-hot pokers bloom among the graves, giving it a charm unique among Skye burial-grounds'. Continue to reach Kilmarie House.

The village of Kilmarie was an early centre of Christianity in Skye and gets its name from St Maolrubha, an obscure missionary saint who established a church here.

The final stretch of the route follows the lovely river up to the main road. Turn left and walk up to the parking area a short distance away.

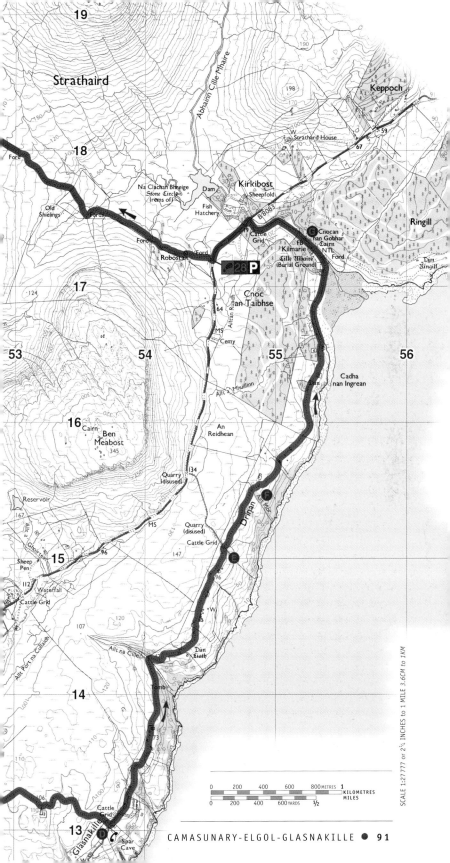

Further Information

 ## *Safety on the Hills*

The hills, mountains and moorlands of Britain, though of modest height compared with those in many other countries, need to be treated with respect. Friendly and inviting in good weather, they can quickly be transformed into wet, misty, windswept and potentially dangerous areas of wilderness in bad weather. Even on an outwardly fine and settled summer day, conditions can rapidly deteriorate at high altitudes and, in winter, even more so.

Therefore it is advisable always to take both warm and waterproof clothing, sufficient nourishing food, a hot drink, first-aid kit, torch and whistle. Wear suitable footwear, such as strong walking boots or shoes that give a good grip over rocky terrain and on slippery slopes. Try to obtain a local weather forecast and bear it in mind before you start. Do not be afraid to abandon your proposed route and return to your starting point in the event of a sudden and unexpected deterioration in the weather. Do not go alone and allow enough time to finish the walk well before nightfall.

Most of the walks described in this book do not venture into remote wilderness areas and will be safe to do, given due care and respect, at any time of year in all but the most unreasonable weather. Indeed, a crisp, fine winter day often provides perfect walking conditions, with firm ground underfoot and a clarity that is not possible to achieve in the other seasons of the year. A few walks, however, are suitable only for reasonably fit and experienced hill walkers able to use a compass and should definitely not be tackled by anyone else during the winter months or in bad weather, especially high winds and mist. These are indicated in the general description that precedes each of the walks.

 ## *Walkers and the Law*

Scotland

Walkers in Scotland have long enjoyed a moral and de facto right of access, now enshrined in *The Land Reform (Scotland) Act 2003*. This carries with it responsibilities, which are outlined in the Scottish Outdoor Access Code. The three key principles are:

- Respect the interests of other people
- Care for the Environment
- Take responsibility for your own actions

The following common situations affect walkers.
- Farm steadings - There is no legal right of access to farm steadings but in practice many existing routes go through them.
- Fields - Keep to paths where possible or walk around the margins of a field under crops.
- Fences, dykes and hedges - When crossing walls, dykes, fences and hedges use a gate or a stile where possible, otherwise climb over carefully to avoid damage.
- Golf Courses - You have a right of access to cross golf courses but must avoid damage to the playing surface and never step on to the greens. Cross as quickly as possible, considering the rights of the players.
- Deer Stalking - During the hunting season check to ensure that the walks you are planning avoid stalking operations.

More detailed information can be obtained at www.outdooraccess-scotland.com.

Glossary of Gaelic Names

Many of the place names in Scotland are Gaelic in origin, and this list gives some of the more common elements, which will allow readers to understand otherwise meaningless words and appreciate the relationship between place names and landscape features. Place names often have variant spellings, and the more common of these are given here.

aber	mouth of loch, river	eilidh	hind
abhainn	river	eòin, eun	bird
allt	stream	fionn	white
auch, ach	field	fraoch	heather
bal, bail, baile	town, homestead	gabhar, ghabhar,	
bàn	white, fair, pale	gobhar	goat
bealach	hill pass	garbh	rough
beg, beag	small	geal	white
ben, beinn	hill	ghlas, glas	grey
bhuidhe	yellow	gleann, glen	narrow, valley
blar	plain	gorm	blue, green
brae, braigh	upper slope, steepening	inbhir, inver	confluence
		inch, inis, innis	island, meadow by river
breac	speckled		
cairn	pile of stones, often marking a summit	lag, laggan	hollow
		làrach	old site
cam	crooked	làirig	pass
càrn	cairn, cairn-shaped hill	leac	slab
		liath	grey
caol, kyle	strait	loch	lake
ceann, ken, kin	head	lochan	small loch
cil, kil	church, cell	màm	pass, rise
clach	stone	maol	bald-shaped top
clachan	small village	monadh	upland, moor
cnoc	hill, knoll, knock	mór, mor(e)	big
coille, killie	wood	odhar, odhair	dun-coloured
corrie, coire,		rhu, rubha	point
choire	mountain hollow	ruadh	red, brown
craig, creag	cliff, crag	sgòr, sgòrr,	
crannog,		sgùrr	pointed
crannag	man-made island	sron	nose
dàl, dail	field, flat	stob	pointed
damh	stag	strath	valley (broader than glen)
dearg	red		
druim, drum	long ridge	tarsuinn	traverse, across
dubh, dhu	black, dark	tom	hillock (rounded)
dùn	hill fort	tòrr	hillock (more rugged)
eas	waterfall	tulloch, tulach	knoll
eilean	island	uisge	water, river

 ## Useful Organisations

Association for the Protection of
Rural Scotland
Gladstone's Land, 3rd floor,
483 Lawnmarket, Edinburgh
EH1 2NT

Tel. 0131 225 7012
www.ruralscotland.btik.com

Forestry Commission
Silvan House, 231 Corstorphine Road,
Edinburgh EH12 7AT
Tel. 0845 3673787
www.forestry.gov.uk

Historic Scotland
Longmore House, Salisbury Place,
Edinburgh EH9 1SH
Tel. 0131 668 8600
www.historic-scotland.gov.uk

The National Trust for Scotland
Hermiston Quay, 5 Cultins Road,
Edinburgh EH11 4DF
Tel. 0844 493 2100
www.nts.org.uk

Ordnance Survey
www.ordnancesurvey.co.uk

Public Transport
Traveline
Tel. 0871 2002233
www.traveline.org.uk

Ramblers Scotland
Kingfisher House,
Auld Mart Business Park,
Milnathort, Kinross
KY13 9DA
Tel. 01577 861 222
www.ramblers.org.uk/scotland

Scottish Natural Heritage
Bridge Road, Portree,
Isle of Skye IV51 9ER
Tel: 01478 613329
www.snh.gov.uk

Scottish Rights of Way and Access Society
24 Annandale Street, Edinburgh
EH7 4AN
Tel. 0131 558 1222
www.scotways.com

Scottish Youth Hostels Association
7 Glebe Crescent, Stirling FK8 2JA
Tel. 01786 891 400
www.syha.org.uk

VisitScotland
Head Office, Ocean Point 1, 94 Ocean Drive,
Leith, Edinburgh EH6 6JH
Tel. 0845 2255 121
www.visitscotland.com

Weather forecasts;
Weathercall - Met Office forecast by phone
(West Highlands and Islands)
Tel: 09068 500 426
www.weathercall.co.uk

 Ordnance Survey maps for Isle of Skye

The walks described in this guide are covered by Ordnance Survey 1:50 000 scale (1¼ inches to 1 mile or 2cm to 1km) Landranger map sheets 23, 32 and 33.

These all-purpose maps are packed with information to help you explore the area. Viewpoints, picnic sites, places of interest and caravan and camping sites are shown, as well as public rights of way information such as footpaths and bridleways.

To examine the area in more detail, especially if you are planning walks, the Ordnance Survey Explorer maps at 1:25 000 scale (2½ inches to 1 mile or 4cm to 1km) are ideal:

407 (Skye – Dunvegan)
408 (Skye – Trotternish & The Storr)
410 (Skye – Portree & Bracadale)
411 (Skye – Cuillin Hills)
412 (Skye: Sleat/Slèite)

To get to the Isle of Skye use the Ordnance Survey Travel Map-Route Great Britain at 1:625 000 (1 inch to 10 miles or 4cm to 25km) scale or Ordnance Survey Road Travel Map-Road 2 (Western Scotland and the Western Isles) at 1:250 000 scale (1 inch to 4 miles or 1cm to 2.5km)

Ordnance Survey maps and guides are available from most booksellers, stationers and newsagents.

Text:	Terry Marsh
Photography:	Terry Marsh, John Brooks and Neil Wilson
Editorial:	Ark Creative (UK) Ltd
Design:	Ark Creative (UK) Ltd

This product includes mapping data licensed from Ordnance Survey® with the permission of the Controller of Her Majesty's Stationery Office. © Crown Copyright 2011. All rights reserved. Licence number 150002047. Ordnance Survey, the OS symbol and Pathfinder are registered trademarks and Explorer, Landranger and Outdoor Leisure are trademarks of the Ordnance Survey, the national mapping agency of Great Britain.

ISBN: 978-1-85458-558-5

While every care has been taken to ensure the accuracy of the route directions, the publishers cannot accept responsibility for errors or omissions, or for changes in details given. The countryside is not static: stiles can change to gates, hedges and fences can be removed, field boundaries can alter, footpaths can be rerouted and changes in ownership can result in the closure or diversion of some concessionary paths. Also, paths that are easy and pleasant for walking in fine conditions may become slippery, muddy and difficult in wet weather, while stepping stones across rivers and streams may become impassable.

If you find an inaccuracy in either the text or maps, please write to Crimson Publishing at the address below.

Printed in Singapore. 1/11

First published in Great Britain 2011 by Crimson Publishing, a division of:
Crimson Business Ltd,
Westminster House, Kew Road, Richmond, Surrey, TW9 2ND

www.totalwalking.co.uk

Front cover: Storr and the Old Man of Storr from Loch Fada
Page 1: Achnaclaich in the south of Skye

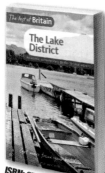